ENCOURAGING STUDENT ENGAGEMENT IN THE BLOCK PERIOD

David Marshak

and

Feather Alexander
Kimberly Allison
Chris Drape
Pat Hegarty
Mark Lovre
Kristi Noren
Jeannie Wenndorf

EYE ON EDUCATION

EYE ON EDUCATION
6 DEPOT WAY WEST, SUITE 106
LARCHMONT, NY 10538
(914) 833–0551
(914) 833–0761 fax

Library of Congress Cataloging-in-Publication Data

Marshak, David
  Encouraging student engagement in the block period / by David Marshak.
      p.   cm.
    ISBN 1-883001-65-X
    1. Block scheduling (Education)—Washington (State)—Seattle Metropolitan Area—Case studies. 2. Action research in education—Washington (State)—Seattle Metropolitan Area—Case studies. 3. High schools—Washington (State)—Seattle Metropolitan Area—Case studies. 4. Education evaluation—Washington (State)—Seattle Metropolitan Area—Case studies. I. Title.
    LB3032.2.M37   1999
    373.12′42′0979772—dc21   98–45146
                                                                        CIP

10 9 8 7 6 5 4 3 2 1

Editorial and production services provided by Richard H. Adin Freelance Editorial Services, 9 Orchard Drive, Gardiner, NY 12525 (914-883-5884)

Other Books on Block Scheduling

Teaching in the Block:
Stategies for Engaging Active Learners
edited by Robert Lynn Canady and Michael D. Rettig

Block Scheduling:
A Catalyst for Change in High Schools
by Robert Lynn Canady and Michael D. Rettig

Middle School Block Scheduling
by Michael D. Rettig and Robert Lynn Canady

The 4 X 4 Block Schedule
by J. Allen Queen and Kimberly Gaskey Isenhour

Action Research on Block Scheduling
by David Marshak

Questions and Answers About Block Scheduling:
An Implementation Guide
by Donald Gainey and John Brucato

Teaching in the Block, the series
Robert Lynn Canady and Michael D. Rettig,
General Editors

Supporting Students with Learning Needs in the Block
by Marcia Conti-D'Antonio, Robert Bertrando,
and Joanne Eisenberger

Teaching Mathematics in the Block
by Susan Gilkey and Carla Hunt

Teaching Foreign Languages in the Block
by Deborah Blaz

For more information on Teaching in the Block, contact us at:

Eye On Education
6 Depot Way West
Larchmont, NY 10538
(914) 833-0551 phone; (914) 833-0761 fax
www.eyeoneducation.com

MEET THE AUTHOR

David Marshak, currently assistant professor at Seattle University, taught in public high schools and alternative high schools in Connecticut and New Hampshire. He received his doctorate in teaching, curriculum, and learning environments from Harvard University Graduate School of Education. He also served as Curriculum and Assessment Coordinator for Addison Northeast school district in Vermont. He is Senior Editor of the hm Learning and Study Skills Programs, published by the National Association of Secondary School Principals, and is the author of *Action Research on Block Scheduling*, also published by Eye On Education.

ACKNOWLEDGMENTS

Many thanks to Fred Bay and the Josephine Bay Paul and C. Michael Paul Foundation for their generous financial support of this research project.

I want to express my admiration for and gratitude toward all of the teacher-researchers that took part in this project.

Thanks to my dean at Seattle University, Dr. Sue Schmitt, for her support of my efforts in this project.

Thanks to Bob Sickles for his continuing engagement with and support of this research.

Thanks to Alan Hall for his very helpful critique of drafts of both this book and the previous one.

TABLE OF CONTENTS

INTRODUCTION

STUDENT ENGAGEMENT IN THE BLOCK PERIOD

This book presents action research studies conducted by seven Seattle area high school teachers in various subject areas, all of whom teach in block periods of 90–105 minutes in length. Each of these teachers works in a high school that has left its traditional moorings and entered into a state of change, transition, and uncertainty. The classrooms described in these studies are not dramatically transformed from the conventional model of twentieth century American high schools, nor do they continue to embody the traditional forms of that model. These classrooms are something different. They include elements of the old conventions as well as elements of exploration and experimentation. These teachers are not radicals. Rather, they are engaged in the process of progressive reform, and their efforts raise the question of whether relatively conventional public high schools can be reinvented for a new era, through a process of gradual change from within.

These seven teachers conducted action research studies about teaching and learning in their own classrooms during the 1996-97 school year. All of these teachers had participated in cooperative action research studies conducted the previous year (published in *Action Research on Block Scheduling* [Eye on Education, 1997]), and so all of them had considerable experience and expertise in the action research process.

I invited each teacher to develop her or his study in terms of this criterion:

> Select the issue or research question that is most significant for you right now in terms of improving your teaching practice.

In response, each of these teacher-researchers developed a study that in some significant way explored the nature and role of student engagement in the block period high school classroom.

As a related set of action research studies, these investigations provide support for several conclusions both about block period teaching and learning, and about action research conducted by schoolteachers.

♦ Effective teaching and learning in block periods both allows and demands a genuine professionalism from teachers.

Kimberly Allison, a teacher at Tahoma High School in Maple Valley, Washington, explains: "Block periods seem to demand that the activities that take place inside the classroom be purposeful and authentic....Meeting for 100 minutes...not only allows for the kind of deep structure experimentation and reflection necessary to expand one's skills as a teacher; it almost demands it....One of the benefits of block periods is the increased sense of accountability for meaningful, effective instruction that most teachers feel in this structure."

Feather Alexander, a teacher at Cedarcrest High School in Duvall, Washington, adds: "The extended block of time not only gave me an opportunity for innovation that a short period would not, but it necessitated this innovation."

♦ Action research has the power to focus teachers on continual improvement through thoughtful innovation, reflection, self-assessment, and revision. A key to this power resides in the capability of data to move teachers from an informal system of self-improvement to a more formal, though still self-controlled, system that is data driven.

Jeannie Wenndorf, a teacher at Lindbergh High School in Renton, Washington, explains: "Gathering data to back up my assumptions was an important step in making solid educational decisions. I felt like a true partner with my students in seeking to understand the value of various assessment strategies. This research has helped me see more clearly what

I do well, and how I can do a better job developing meaningful, engaging assessment tools in the years to come."

Feather Alexander notes: "The excitement of the study was that it was designed to work within the context of my classroom, and it was developed to promote my growth and improvement as a teacher. The study was undertaken to see if my idea for restructuring roles and time in a block period class would work. And the result would be to tell the story of what went on within my classroom with the hopes that it would inform my practice."

Mark Lovre, a teacher at Cedarcrest High School, explains: "What I've learned from this study is that there are clearly many ways that I can improve my classroom system. My primary focus will be on assessment. I need to clarify the objectives for each project in each unit and tie these together more effectively across the entire course. This clarification will allow me to use these objectives to create clear and meaningful rubrics for all of the projects. Better rubrics will allow the students to work more meaningfully and learn better."

- ♦ There is significant learning available to teachers who choose to pay serious, careful attention to what students think and feel about their teaching. These teachers can gain access to such learning through the purposeful collection of data from their students and from the analysis and consideration of these data.

Chris Drape, a teacher at Lindbergh High School, explains: "Perhaps the clearest message I received from the research is the value of interviewing my students and treating their analyses of our classroom with respect."

Probably the most significant conclusion is this:

- ♦ The block period in high school provides an environment which allows and supports teaching and learning activities that can both increase student engagement and generate and nurture student initiative and responsibility.

Kimberly Allison explored the procedures for and value of engaging students in developing their own assessment tools in a speech class and in applying these assessment tools to their own speeches and group discussions. With guidance and support from Allison, students heightened their engagement in the class as they first developed standards for judging their own performance and learning and then applied these standards to themselves and their peers. When students helped to develop the standards for measuring their own work, they displayed a greater sense of responsibility for the quality of that work. (See Chapter 1.)

Jeannie Wenndorf researched the comparison between tests and *project assessments* in her Biology classes. A project assessment, in her definition, is a student-developed project that gives students an opportunity to synthesize and apply major concepts that they learned in a unit. Project assessments generated a high level of engagement for many students and encouraged them to take initiative as they created complex projects that demonstrated their comprehension of the unit's material. (See Chapter 2.)

Mark Lovre investigated how he could organize his classroom and curriculum in his junior and senior literature classes so as to promote students' learning of content and skills simultaneously with students' development of increased responsibility, initiative, and self-management. Lovre's classroom system gave students a wide range of freedom, which both demanded that students take greater responsibility and initiative and encouraged students to learn how to operate more effectively with increased independence from the teacher's direct control of their time and behavior. Lovre found that many of his students became more able to manage their use of time as they worked within his class, and that many still struggled with multiple, simultaneous assignments. He also learned that as students became more skilled in employing their in-class work time, they became more engaged in the life of the class. (See Chapter 3.)

Feather Alexander explored the ways in which she could involve her students as teachers of each other within her block-period classroom. Her enlisting of her students into teaching roles required them to accept greater responsibility for their own learning and to take greater initiative in relation to enacting their new role of peer teacher. As students learned to be more successful as teachers of their peers, they chose to become more engaged in the entire array of activities in this classroom. (See Chapter 4.)

Kristi Noren experimented with providing her personal-fitness class students with more specific data about their own health and fitness and with involving them in personalized goal setting and individualized training programs. The objective was to see if they would become more engaged in the class' activities. Given more specific personal goals and training programs and more detailed feedback, Noren found that almost all of her students did indeed increase their level of engagement in the class. Many chose to take more initiative in regard to their exercise levels and became more committed to their exercise regimen. (See Chapter 5.)

Chris Drape investigated the depth versus coverage dilemma in U.S. History by involving his students in an in-depth project about the Vietnam War era that included the study of multiple text sources and an interview of an adult who lived during the Vietnam War. His study focused on the issue of student engagement when students experienced themselves as active learners in the block-period classroom. Drape found that his students were more engaged, cared about their learning more, and created better products when they were involved as "historians" rather than just as receivers of information. (See Chapter 6.)

In his ninth-grade English class, Pat Hegarty found the writing workshop to be the most effective activity for the kinds of learning and productivity demanded by the assignment of a literary essay based on *Romeo and Juliet*. Hegarty reached the conclusion that the power of the writing workshop lay in the "almost complete though organized freedom" it offers to students. He explained, "...at least to some extent, the more independence I allowed, the greater the effectiveness of the strategy, both in the mind of the adolescent and in the view of the instructor." In this study, structured freedom led to the greatest amount of student engagement. (See Chapter 7.)

The common structure employed by all of these teachers was the simultaneous and interrelated provision to students of increased independence from direct adult control and increased responsibility. Each of these teachers wanted more from students: more engagement, more caring about learning, more effort, more willingness to be responsible, more initiative. Each offered students more: more choice, more control, more respect for their interests and capabilities, more collaborative effort and common cause. To a significant extent, the majority of students in each of these studies accepted the new arrangements offered by their teachers and performed as learners at new levels of engagement, initiative, accomplishment, and sophistication, as perceived by all of the teachers and most of the students engaged in these studies.

The key idea to emerge from these studies is that block periods have the potential to encourage high school teachers to re-vision their perceptions of their adolescent students' capacities for engagement, responsibility and initiative, and for constructive independence and interdependence. At the same time, the 80–100 minutes in the block period provide teachers and students with the learning context in which these new student roles and capacities—and new teacher roles—can be enacted.

These seven studies demonstrate the efforts of thoughtful teacher-researchers at work. They are models for how to conduct the action research process in one's own classroom while teaching a full load of high school classes. They provide immediately useful insights into block-period teaching and learning. Further, they demonstrate the potential for generating learning experiences in high school block period classes that teach young people the values and the skills of engagement, initiative, and responsibility needed for successful adult behavior in the family, the community, the workplace, and in civic and democratic life.

Each study is followed by a brief commentary, *Ideas for Next Steps*, which suggests specific ways in which each teacher could continue to develop and improve the efforts she or he has described in that study.

The final chapter, Chapter 8, explores the insights and understandings suggested by these seven studies about how teachers can promote student engagement in high school block period classes.

1

STUDENT-DEVELOPED ASSESSMENT AND STUDENT SELF-ASSESSMENT IN BLOCK PERIODS

Kimberly Allison
Tahoma High School

In her speech class, Kimberly Allison used the block period structure to explore both the utility of student-developed assessment tools for speeches and group discussions and students' self-assessment of their speeches and discussions using these tools. Allison engaged her students in developing the evaluative criteria for effective public speaking and then in applying these criteria to their own performances.

Block periods gave her the time required for this work. But were the outcomes worth the investment of time needed?

Yes, she explains, "The somewhat sloppy process of arriving at this finished product was worth the time and effort. Students really knew what was expected of them in a class discussion." Later Allison describes the ways in which most of her students became more effective learners as they worked to achieve standards of speech performance which they had helped to articulate.

INTRODUCTION

Among other courses, I teach a semester-long elective speech course at Tahoma High School, a rural and suburban high school twenty miles southeast of Seattle. Three years ago, in 1994, we adopted a block period schedule. Students take 6 classes each semester; each class meets every other day for 103 minutes. Block periods have allowed me to examine the issues all teachers face but have little time to ponder. For instance, I began teaching the speech course 4 years ago in traditional 55-minute periods and have struggled with the same issues of assessment and teaching methodology each year. Over the last three years I have experimented with assessment and instruction in deliberate and meaningful ways because block periods seem to demand that the activities that take place inside the classroom be purposeful and authentic. Gone are the days of winging it.

Four years ago I had had no previous formal instruction in or experience with speech. My experience was limited to the speaking I did myself, which was mostly limited to class presentations and student teaching. Having never taken a speech class myself, I was unsure at first just how I was qualified to teach it. I am sure that some of my struggle with assessment stems from my reluctance to teach and grade what I myself have not done. Before I started teaching and assessing writing, I considered myself a writer. Before I started teaching and assessing reading, I considered myself a reader. Over the four years that I have taught speech, I have become much more comfortable with myself as "speech teacher," but assessment still concerns me.

My philosophy tends to focus on process over product, which works well with a writing workshop approach to writing instruction. In contrast, this emphasis doesn't appear to be as effective in speech class, where the assessment of speech demands a greater emphasis on the product. I want assessment to be meaningful and accurate, and yet traditional end-product assessment often seems to undermine my goals for the class. I also want students to improve over the course of the quarter. Grading each individual speech with a letter or number grade does not contribute to the classroom climate of growth that I'm trying to create. Over the years I've tried grading on improvement, which is simply too subjective and requires a keen memory of past speeches and/or vast quantities of notes. I've also experimented with a check, plus, and minus system for documenting the student's meeting, exceeding, or failing to meet certain assignment criteria. Nothing that I've tried has really met my goals for assessing and promoting student improvement over time. Thus, when we began the block-period schedule, I started to experiment with some student self-assessment of speeches.

Why did this experimentation start with the advent of block periods? Meeting for 100 minutes every other day not only allows for the kind of deep-structure experimentation and reflection necessary to expand one's skills as a teacher— it demands it. One of the benefits of block periods is the increased sense of accountability for meaningful, effective instruction that most teachers feel in this structure. In a similar vein, students in block periods are often looking for more meaningful assessment and feedback from teachers. It's as though the extended time we spend together every other day (even though it's technically the same total amount of time per year) seems to make everything that happens in the classroom feel more important. Students are more demanding, which provides teachers with a great opportunity to engage students with meaningful and purposeful instruction.

Experimenting with student self-assessment the last couple of years, I often put the cart before the horse, because I asked students to assess themselves using criteria that I had established myself but had not always shared with them before they did the assignment. Therefore, I often felt discour-

aged with the results of their self-assessments and was unsure of the value of taking the time for self-assessment. My
main objective in speech is for students to discover what they
need to do to improve. I feel that if I give them the criteria for
a good speech up front, students are less likely to engage in
the kind of self-discovery that can be so valuable for them.

While beginning to develop my research question, I was
involved in an assessment institute that was offered to district teachers and taught by our district curriculum coordina-
tors/developers. My involvement in this institute, with its focus on meaningful and reflective assessment practices, led
me to think about student-developed assessment combined
with self-assessment. In our district, student self-assessment
is an accepted and encouraged assessment tool. However, I
was often unsure of its accuracy and validity. Philosophically,
I wanted to embrace the importance of metacognition and
student self-assessment; but I had many questions: Were students simply demonstrating their skill at telling us what we
as teachers wanted to hear? Was the reflection students were
doing actually meaningful to them, and was this self-assessment something on which I could base a grade?

The idea of working with students to develop rubrics and
other grading criteria was relatively new to me. However, as I
listened to one experienced language arts teacher explain
how her students work with her in developing the criteria for
an assignment, determining due dates, and self-evaluating
the project at its conclusion, this approach made sense to me.
I decided to combine her practice with an assessment tool I
had started to use the year before with limited success.

Last year I began a new system of assessing student
speeches. Students were required to record all of their
speeches given in class on videotape. After delivering and recording their speech, students were required to view their
tape at home, to use a self-reflection tool to assess their
strengths and weaknesses regarding both the content and delivery of their speech, and to set personal goals for their next
speech. I then reviewed these reflections and assigned points
for completeness and for supporting detail. In many cases,
specific supporting details were insufficient, and I began to
worry that the grade students received was a reflection of

their ability to self-assess, not of their speaking ability. I believed in the power of watching oneself on videotape; but I realized that many students simply made up their self-reflection without viewing their tape.

This year I wanted to continue to employ videotapes, but I hoped for greater success. I realized that the self-reflection form I had been using was long and perhaps overwhelming. It asked students to reflect on all areas of their speech instead of concentrating on the few main areas that we had discussed in class prior to the particular speech they were reviewing. I hypothesized that if the students contributed to the development of the criteria for the speech and if the self-reflection/ assessment mirrored these criteria, perhaps students would take more interest and ownership in viewing their video-taped speeches and completing the self-assessment.

RESEARCH QUESTIONS

The process of reflection described above led me to these research questions:

- ◆ Student-developed assessment and student self-assessment take more class time to develop and implement than our block-period schedule allows. Is the extra class time that student-developed assessment and student self-assessment take worthwhile?

- ◆ Does student-developed assessment aid students' understanding and learning of key concepts?

- ◆ Are student self-assessments an accurate reflection of student learning/achievement? (I also wondered how student self-assessments compared with my own assessment of the same speech.)

- ◆ Finally, how are the students' expectations and standards for their own performance affected by student-developed assessments and student self-assessments?

THE ENVIRONMENT

Generally, the students who register for my speech course are self-motivated and interested in speech. However, at least a few students each year are placed in the class as a result of scheduling conflicts rather than choice. I chose to conduct my research in this particular class because of my interest in meaningful assessment in speech. Additionally, we were just beginning the actual speaking component of the class. The timing was perfect.

We were approximately six weeks into the semester and had spent that time working on *personal profiles*, a unit in which students explored and discovered who they are socially, emotionally, economically, and so forth, and how their values are shaped by those around them. Activities included informal papers, collages, and poems. The objective was for students to gain a better understanding of who they are and of who and what they represent and, thereby, to develop more self-esteem and confidence when speaking in public.

I began my research as we were wrapping up this unit. In fact, the first speech that students made to the class was the presentation of a part of their personal profile, which I discuss in detail later. Concurrently, I was introducing the concept of group discussion, which is one of the units I teach in this speech class. I had decided to set aside Fridays for focused group discussions. I describe the group discussion component of the class first because it was our first attempt at student-developed assessment, and what I learned watching students struggle with student-developed assessment and student self-assessment for group discussions was valuable.

GROUP DISCUSSION

In addition to giving individual speeches, students were required to participate in whole-group discussions, which occurred almost every time the class met on a Friday. This worked out to be about every other week because we are on a revolving A-B schedule. These discussion days consisted of me giving the group a current article from the newspaper that highlighted a relevant controversy, such as curfews or parental versus teenage rights. Students read the article silently and were asked to highlight important and interesting details. As they concluded their reading, I asked them to free-write their reaction to the article. If necessary, I offered them a question to get them started. This personal writing assured that everyone would have something to contribute to the conversation. Students were then involved in discussing the issues in the article while sitting in a large circle.

OUR FIRST DISCUSSION

For our first discussion I gave students no rules. We simply began after they had had time to read the article and complete the free-write. I did, however, ask two students to sit out the discussion and act as observers. I asked them to take notes concerning types of behaviors they observed that helped the group discussion and those that appeared to sidetrack, distract from, or stall it. I also sat outside the group and took similar notes.

What the two observers and I noticed was not surprising. Five students of the fifteen present dominated the discussion. One particularly vocal and opinionated female student was repeatedly the target of an equally vocal and opinionated male student's personal attacks. A couple of times the discussion started to wander into territory not directly related to the topic. Students talked over other students; comments seldom had any connection to the previous comment. Often, comments relied on speculative information rather than on information found in the article. Students rarely used facts and details from the article to support their opinions. One student-observer noted how difficult it was for him to stay out of the discussion when students said things that simply weren't true, or at least had no basis in the article they had just read. In short, it was a free-for-all, and it only came to an end when I stepped in, brought closure, and transitioned to a teacher-led conversation about group dynamics.

After this conversation, which lasted for twenty minutes, I asked the students to reflect on how they thought the previous group discussion had gone. The comments students offered ranged from the ambiguous, "It was okay," to the vocal male student trying again to attack the vocal female student. In the middle, students made comments that the discussion seemed to be dominated by the vocal pair, that it was hard to stay on the topic, and that they were frustrated because they did not have more guidance from me. As this discussion continued, I asked the two student-observers to comment on what they had seen in general terms, without names. These students shared the same observations I mentioned earlier.

At this point, I asked students to describe what would have made the discussion more successful. Their suggestions included: participation from all, not just a few students; sticking to the topic and using the article as a reference when necessary; letting well-reasoned facts guide the discussion instead of emotionally charged opinion; and eliminating personal attacks. I wrote all of these suggestions on the board.

For homework I asked students to create the criteria for a class discussion rubric. I distributed a blank rubric form (Appendix 1.1, p. 27) that I had acquired at the assessment institute I attended and asked them to create at least three criteria for each level of performance. I suggested that students start with the "capable" level, then work up and down from there. We spent some time discussing the vocabulary on the sheet and brainstorming possible criteria.

When students returned to class with their completed (or incomplete) rubrics, I realized that I had jumped the gun. While I was confident these students knew what type of participation contributed to a successful discussion, it became apparent that transferring this knowledge to a scoring rubric was beyond their present ability. Most students had difficulty creating meaningful distinctions between the levels in the rubric. For instance, many students established some criteria for verbal participation in a discussion. During the preceding class period we had considered this question, and we had noted that establishing a quantifiable criterion, such as "participated five or more times" seemed to be ineffective. Discussions may call for more or less participation from individual students, and this type of criterion neglected the quality of the participation. With a criterion like this, an individual student could speak five times but offer little insight to the discussion. Also, students who unfairly dominated a discussion would be awarded the same score as someone whose participation was balanced and allowed for others to contribute. As a result, students could only use vague modifiers such as *a lot*, *often*, *sometimes*, or *frequently*. Not surprisingly, students were struggling with the same issues teachers struggle with when trying to make assessment fair, meaningful, and accurate.

As I realized the error of my ways, I backed up and asked students to review their rubrics to find the elements or components for which they had attempted to create criteria. I collected these on the overhead as students shared. Once the list was complete, we worked with the listed items to form categories. These included:

- participation (quantity)
- content (argumentation, knowledge/preparation of subject, sticking to the topic)
- presentation (tone of voice, body language, eye contact, volume, emotion)
- respect (interaction with others/taking turns, listening, attacking arguments instead of people).

This last category seemed to be an element of the three other categories (especially presentation), but students felt that it deserved a category of its own.

At this point, I was pleased. If we were having trouble creating a rubric, at least students were discussing important elements of group discussions. I then broke students into four groups and asked each group to develop the specific criteria for one of the four categories we had created. This task appeared to be easier for students because they were creating a descriptive sentence that explained the behavior required for each level of performance. These sentences included the elements or components we had listed as a class. Once groups created their criteria, they shared their minirubrics with the whole group via overhead transparencies. As each group presented its conclusions, the large group continued to shape and refine the criteria. Once this process was completed, I had my student teaching assistant compile and type up the criteria we decided on as a class.

The completed rubric, while not perfect, served as an assessment tool for future discussions. The somewhat sloppy process of arriving at this finished product was worth the time and effort. Students really knew what was expected of them in a class discussion. Furthermore, they began to realize the intricacies of a successful discussion. For instance, not all participation is verbal; nodding appropriately, making eye contact with participants, and careful listening also contribute. Thus we had successfully completed our first adventure in student-developed assessment.

OUR SECOND DISCUSSION

Student self-assessment using the rubric was another matter. The first discussion we had using the rubric was disheartening to me. I anticipated that students would use the rubric to self-assess in an accurate and timely manner, saving me time in generating and recording grades. The discussion format was the same as before. I sat outside the group while students participated in the discussion. As the discussion unfolded, I made marks by each student's name as he or she participated. Comments that sidetracked or subverted the discussion were noted by a minus sign. Students knew I was marking participation in such a manner.

While watching the discussion, I observed that one student kept looking to me for guidance or approval. It was difficult for him to engage fully in the discussion while simultaneously attending to my reaction to what he was saying. Throughout the initial course of this research, I noticed that students often had difficulty trusting in their own perceptions and judgments of how well they were doing. All too often I felt that the students believed that I held some sort of ultimate objective standard that they were to try to attain.

At the end of the discussion I asked students to use the rubric to rate themselves. I explained that in each area (participation, content, presentation, and respect), they were to determine which number/level best reflected their participation and then to explain why they deserved this grade. To my surprise and disappointment three students radically misrepresented their participation. I noticed this as I was glancing through their self-assessments before students actually left the classroom. I called these students over and asked if they could explain to me how they could have earned a four in participation when my records showed nothing. Two of these students were in this class not by choice but by scheduling constraints. They were already failing for lack of participation in the class, and they simply harrumphed, said "Whatever," and walked out. This behavior was consistent with their lack of interest in everything we had done in class so far. The third student, however, tried to argue that he had participated— but with the two students just mentioned, not the whole group. He felt his note passing and side comments should count for something. I explained that his interpretation of the scoring criteria was stretching its actual definition, and he conceded the truth of this comment. Upon reflection, I believe this last student was either testing the system to see what he could get away with or testing me. For the rest of the semester, his self-assessments were accurate.

The remaining students' self-assessments corresponded with what I felt was an accurate level. Some students were harder on themselves than I would have been; others supported their score with information that I would not have originally considered. Overall, I believe that this first attempt at student-developed and self-assessments was a success because the great majority of students applied the assessment tool accurately and effectively.

SURVEYING THE STUDENTS

After my students had had the experience of creating and using their own rubric, I explained my research project to them and asked them to fill out a survey (Appendix 1.2, p. 28) regarding their attitudes and experiences with student-developed assessments and self-assessment. The first question asked students about the value of student-developed assessment tools. All but three of the eighteen students responding saw great value in student-developed assessments. As one student wrote:

> Yes, they are valuable…because the students know exactly what's expected of them, and it causes more thought about the process (of the assignment)

> before it begins. Students often make more critical rubrics than the teacher, and 30 students (normal class size) could very easily have good ideas that the teacher never thought of.

Many students made similar comments, especially about students generating ideas and criteria that the teacher might not have developed alone. Many students commented on how student-developed assessments made it easier to learn the material, and one noted that students were more likely to recall criteria and rules that they had personally created. The students who did not see value in student-developed assessments affirmed one of my greatest concerns: that students will set lower, less challenging standards for themselves if they think they can. One student explained, "No, I find that often the assessments are either purposely made easy or the students just try to list everything they think the teacher will want to hear." Another student commented, "With student-developed assessments students will generally make a standard which is easily attainable, therefore, not being challenged."

Student responses to the second question concerning the accuracy of student-developed assessments were more varied. Most students believed that they were accurate; however, more students offered conditions as elements of their responses. Some students commented that the accuracy was dependent on the assessment tool. One student explained:

> It depends on the assessment developed whether or not it is accurate. People many times set goals or expectations for themselves that are unattainable, but it also allows them to work harder for an achievement. On the other hand, people cheat themselves by making goals or expectations that are easy to obtain.

This comment again raised my fears.

In response to question three, all students reported that student-developed assessments helped them and peers learn the material to some extent. No student felt that student-developed assessments were of little or no help. One student commented, "Yes, it makes students have to try harder to get the grade they want and they know how to get it." Another student mentioned that student-developed assessments shifted the emphasis from *the teacher giving the grade* to *the student earning the grade* because the student actually understood the material to be mastered and the criteria on which her or his performance would be graded.

These first three survey questions identified the advantages of student-developed assessments in ways meaningful to teachers and students alike. The experiences I describe below correspond well with this initial data. Nonetheless, when students were asked about the class time it takes to develop student-developed assessments, responses were more varied. While the majority of students thought the time investment was worth it, three students definitely said it was not. A fairly traditional response from a student who did not support student-developed assessments in any of the preceding questions was this: "No, the teacher is supposed to be teaching us what we are supposed to learn. It [student-developed assessment] gives the attitude 'I [the teacher] can't decide what I want to teach so why don't you students decide for me.'"

Another student explained that he thought the time could be better spent on individuals in need of help. The students who felt the time devoted to student-developed assessments was worthwhile expressed a variety of reasons for this value: "Yes, if something will aid the learning, it really doesn't matter how much time it takes, one shouldn't hamper learning because of a time limit." "It [student-developed assessment] will get the kids more involved in the class. It also lets the kids know what it would be like to be the teacher—letting the kids know the teacher's position." And finally, "I believe it's worth it. That way the kids learn more about the whole experience, instead of just the work part of it."

The fifth question asked about students' prior experience with student-developed assessments. Most students had not had any experience with this alternative assessment practice. However, the two students who'd had prior experience with student-developed assessments and student self-assessments were also currently enrolled or had been enrolled in our school's integrated science, language arts, and social studies program. The senior who had participated in the Integrated program two years earlier was a strong advocate of student-developed assessment; however, the sophomore currently enrolled in the program was skeptical of student-developed assessment.

The advantages of student-developed assessment that students mentioned, which are listed here, often echoed points they had mentioned earlier:

- gets everyone involved
- helps everyone understand the guidelines
- helps students learn the entire area they are studying
- builds on students' prior knowledge
- students know what is expected
- critical thinking
- gives students the chance to express their views
- allows room for creativity
- students participate in creating the criteria
- everything is fair
- doesn't allow for any student excuses

Finally, the disadvantages noted by students, which are listed here, also reflected concerns identified previously:

- students may set lower, less challenging standards
- wastes time
- information might not be as good or accurate
- students may not have enough information about the topic/skill to create criteria

The most frequent negative comments made concerned the potential for lower standards and the time student-developed assessment requires.

Overall, student reaction to student-developed assessments was positive at the time of this initial survey. The concerns expressed about lower standards, use of time, and that student-developed assessments might be missing some information that only the teacher could provide, seemed to become less of an issue as the semester continued and students gained more experience with student-developed assessment and student self-assessment.

SPEECH MAKING

At the same time that students were creating their discussion rubrics, they also presented their personal profiles to the class as the conclusion of the introductory unit. As with the first whole-class discussion, I gave students little in the way of instruction preceding their presentations. I simply asked students to prepare to present and share one aspect of their profile with the class. On the day students presented, I asked each student to divide a blank sheet of paper in half and label one side "positive behaviors" and the other "negative behaviors." I then asked the students to record all the positive and negative behaviors they noticed as they watched each other's presentations.

The presentations took only about half of the period. Interest was high, and students were busily noting the positive and negative characteristics they observed. After the presentations, we created a master list of common characteristics on the board. My prior experience with the discussion rubric made me slow down at this stage. I simply typed up this list and distributed it during the following class period.

When I assigned their next speech, I asked students to select two of the positive characteristics from the list we had generated which they were to incorporate into their speech, and one negative behavior to avoid, along with a rationale for each selection. As another element in the assignment, each student was required to videotape his or her speech when it was presented in class. After giving and taping their speeches, students were instructed to watch their tape at home and write a brief reflection based on their earlier goal setting for this speech. Additionally, students were instructed to set goals for their next speech based on what they determined needed improvement in this speech. This initial step of looking for positive and negative characteristics appeared to help students become clearer about the subtleties of good speech making. These reflections and all similar comments went into each students' portfolio to be used later when students self-assessed for the quarter.

After this initial experience, we began to get more specific. We went back to our preliminary list and added to it. Students started noticing obvious categories of characteristics so we worked on determining the categories. Three emerged: content, delivery, and visual aids. These three areas became the focus for the rest of the semester. At first we simply had a categorized list. Students continued to set goals, give speeches, and reflect using this list of speech components.

As students became comfortable with these three components and the few characteristics we had listed for each, I began pushing them to develop more specific criteria. Over the next few days we started making notes. I say *making* instead of *taking* because they truly were constructing the notes. I was working from a detailed model rubric another teacher had lent me so that I could make sure that we covered the essential areas within each component. We began with content, then delivery, and finished with visual aids. The notes we made were created when I asked students questions such as: "What's the first thing a speaker needs to do at the beginning of his or her speech?" Student responses to this question engaged us in talking about getting the audience's attention and preparing them for a topic. Students quickly realized that this was similar to what they had been taught in writing, and so they patterned the rest of the content component for speeches after what they knew about good writing.

We engaged in the same sort of note making for each speech component. I was astounded by how much these students knew! They were creating the notes themselves; I was merely the secretary who occasionally asked probing and/or clarifying questions. Unlike other times when I had given students notes on the very same information, students were fully engaged. They were discovering and processing the information in a much more meaningful way. Because they were creating the notes, the traditional "checking for understanding" was built in, not tacked onto the lesson.

Even though each note-making session with discussion took a whole class period, for me, as their teacher, the whole experience was very liberating. Instead of focusing on the *what* of speaking, I could step back and let the students discuss and generate the *how* and *why* of speaking, processing the information at a much higher level. At the end of one of our note-making sessions, I didn't worry about whether or not they had "gotten it." I knew they had!

I typed up our outlines for speech content and delivery (I saved the visual aid component for a later time when we would be using such aids) in a user-friendly format. Students then used this list to set specific content and delivery goals. We experimented with a variety of self-reflection/assessment tools to use with their videotapes: checklists (plus, check, minus); general goal-setting/reflection; mapping of speech behaviors over the length of the speech; and answering questions specifically related to the assigned speech. Overall, I began to be more impressed by my students' ability to cite specific details in their post-speech reflection activity regardless of what tool we used.

Because these tools were meant to be instructive and because I didn't want students' grades to be primarily a reflection of their ability to self-assess, I held off grading the tools themselves and simply offered comments where I saw a need for more detail. The students' reflections and any comments I made during their speech went into their portfolios. I recorded check marks in my grade book when speeches and activities were completed. I did not assign letter or numerical grades to individual speeches or reflections. Sometimes one of our tools might ask students to assign a grade to their speech, but what I was interested in was their support for that grade as opposed to the grade itself.

At the end of the quarter, I asked students to look through and reflect upon their portfolios. I gave them a reflection tool that asked them to describe their growth in planning, preparing, and giving their speeches; explain their greatest struggle and success; and assign the letter grade that best reflected their participation, preparedness, growth, and improvement over the quarter, supported by evidence and examples. Finally, students were asked to set three specific goals for the following quarter.

In previous classes, I had asked students to reflect and self-assess at the end of a quarter, knowing that I would adjust grades whenever I felt it necessary. However, never before had I decided what grade I would give to each student *before* I read her or his self-assessment. This time that's just what I did. I was a bit afraid that I'd find out that the accuracy component of my research question was about to be answered in the negative. Whether students would assess too high or too low, I didn't know. In fact, I expected both. I didn't expect to be right on with all but three students. Even students with whom I kept wavering on their grade expressed the same uncertainty and grade range in their reflections. Of the three students whose self-assessments were different from mine, all scored themselves a letter grade higher. However, because their rationale was specific, I was convinced in two cases to split the difference with them and average my grade with their own. In the other case, the student's rationale and evidence were weak, and I stuck with my initial grade and made numerous comments supporting my decision.

I found this method of checks and balances both efficient and successful. Students benefited from the critical thinking required to self-assess successfully. I enjoyed the process of assessing their grade and then comparing mine to theirs. Because I had taken the time to assess their progress and improvement before looking at their self-assessments, I had my own rationale clearly developed before being swayed by theirs and was able to reconsider and compromise when necessary.

SECOND QUARTER

The second quarter proceeded with a variety of speeches and the application of various assessment tools, such as rubrics, checklists, and narrative summaries, all developed by the students and then put to use. After a couple of speeches a pattern began to develop that seemed to work well. I began by providing the essential specifications of the speech assignment. For instance, when I assigned demonstration speeches, I began by telling students that the speech would have to demonstrate a process, be delivered with note cards, and be three to five minutes long. After I had provided these specifications, we devoted some class time to brainstorming possible topics and approaches that were appropriate to the assigned speech. For homework, students were assigned some beginning tasks such as selecting a topic and collecting source material. When we reconvened as a class, students were prepared to discuss the nuts and bolts of how the speeches would be assessed. This seemed like the right time to discuss the assessment tool; students had had the opportunity to discuss and work with the essential elements of the speech, and yet it was early enough in the speech process for the design of assessment to have a significant impact on the students' work.

Overall, our experiment with student-developed assessments and student self-assessments went smoothly during the second quarter. However, one group project had to be repeated as a result of the students' inaccurate self-assessments. The assignment had been to create and present a commercial promoting our school. Students worked in self-selected groups of four for this activity. I followed the procedure laid out earlier for the most part and allowed students one full class period to work on their commercials because it was a group project. Students developed criteria for a C, B, and A commercial, and we all agreed that any group not meeting the requirements for at least a C should be required to redo the commercial. As groups presented their commercials, the other students and I assessed them using our student-developed checklist. After watching each group's commercial, I was disappointed to see that all of the groups had failed in some respect to meet the minimum requirements for a C and would thus have to redo their commercials. I was further disappointed that none of the groups in their assessments of the other commercials or in their self-assessments of their own work recognized or acknowledged their deficiencies. In fact, I was baffled. Our checklist clearly indicated that visual aids and a positive spin were necessary for the C. Either or both were missing in every commercial.

As we discussed this dilemma, we all began to realize how often students are not held accountable for the stated minimum requirements. I readily admitted that all the commercials were fun and creative and, indeed, were fine examples of commercials. However, they didn't meet the requirements on which we had decided, and I was determined to hold my students accountable to these requirements. To my surprise, they didn't make much of a fuss. The anger and disappointment they felt was directed at the assessment tool, not at me. To remedy the situation, we spent the first part of the next period reworking the assessment tool. To my surprise, not much changed. I thought they might try to throw out the requirements for visual aids and a positive focus, but they didn't. Instead they talked about what appropriate and adequate visual aids were. Then they had a much-needed discussion about the difference between satire and school bashing. After this, students were much clearer about the expectations. Their second round of commercials all succeeded at the A or B level.

This experience, though time-consuming, was very productive because it really drove home how much power the assessment tool itself has. If I create the assessment tool independent of student input, then students are likely to perceive it as lacking connection to their own understanding and/or as lacking meaning. If, on the other hand, students help to generate the tool and then use it themselves, they are much more likely to accept and value the criteria and to do what it takes to achieve them. In addition, the connection between the work they do and the grade they receive becomes clear to them, because they have articulated the expectations themselves, at least to a significant extent.

END OF SEMESTER SURVEY AND CONCLUSION

At the end of the semester I asked students to fill out another survey (Appendix 1.3, p. 29) to capture their response to student-developed assessments and student self-assessments after they had spent most of the semester working with them. I was afraid I might discover that what at the beginning of the semester had been positive reactions, might have changed to negative, given how much we had struggled with student-developed assessments. Indeed, student-developed assessments and student self-assessments do require more work and thought from students. However, I was not disappointed.

I first asked students to reflect on the pros and cons of the alternative assessment tools we had used in regard to their own learning. I wanted them to focus on the impact student-developed assessments and student self-assessments had on their learning because by this time I realized that if there were a positive impact, then the extra time was worth it. The pros far outweighed the cons. However, one particular con surfaced again and again: students were often uncertain what their grade was during the course of the quarter. They expressed the need for specific letter grades or percentages along the way. Even though students had been watching each speech given in class on videotape and thoroughly self-assessing each one, they still did not feel entirely confident in knowing how they were doing. One student said, "You really don't know how well you are doing as far as grades." Ironically, the same student wrote in the pro column: "You get specifics of what you did right and exactly what you did wrong. A letter grade is so general and really doesn't tell you what to do." Many students echoed both of these students' remarks and made it clear to me that while they appreciated the meaningfulness of student-developed assessments and student self-assessments, there was still a desperate need for what one student called "solid info—a grade."

After reading their pros and cons, I thought the second question would show my students' desire for letter grades even more strongly. Interestingly, only two of the fourteen students surveyed at the end of the semester answered yes to whether or not they would have preferred teacher-developed and teacher-graded assessments. One student responded, "No, I would not have preferred to have had letter grades. The reason being is that speaking is harder for some than it is for others. You really can't give someone a bad grade because they are shy and have a hard time speaking." Another student wrote, "No, it helps to understand, create, and know your own expectations. In addition to self-grading, it lets you see for yourself what needs to change."

Only one student suggested that this method had empowered her: "I can also estimate my grades with confidence and not be surprised at the end of the semester." After reading this comment, I realized that this was truly one of my goals with student-developed assessments and student self-assessments. I wanted students to move away from traditional letter grades and to pay attention to what they need to learn and practice so that they can improve. The real goal in speech is to become a confident and competent speaker, not to earn a specific letter grade. I believe that we began working toward this goal but have a way to go before students are willing to place more emphasis on meaningful assessments and less on letter grades. Next year I will do more work, specifically addressing the question of what grades really tell us, in my attempt to get students to see the value of what they are learning when they develop and use their own assessments. I do believe students valued what they were learning, as the comments above suggest; however, they still needed that learning validated by a letter grade from me.

I think part of this problem could be remedied if I gave more feedback to my students. Many students commented in the "what could be improved" section that they would have liked more feedback from me. I had not purposefully withheld my feedback, but had only offered comments that affirmed their own or that brought up issues worthy of consideration which I thought they had overlooked in their own assessments. Looking back, I think students thought I possessed some data or evaluations that I was not sharing with them. If we had addressed this issue earlier in the semester, perhaps students would have felt more confident and comfortable with the assessments they, and I, were using.

Block periods allowed me to experiment with assessment in meaningful and purposeful ways that would not have been possible in traditional fifty-minute periods. In fact, the block periods demanded it. Block periods provided both the impetus and the environment for my research. The concentration of time spent with students made assessment issues I had struggled with in the past come to a head. Block periods demand more of teachers and students alike, and thus I believe they will continue to compel educators to carefully reflect upon and refine their instructional and assessment methods.

IDEAS FOR NEXT STEPS

In this study Kimberly Allison describes her efforts to promote student engagement and learning by involving students in developing rubrics based on their own collective insight and understanding about skillful participation in class discussions and about effective speech making. Both Allison and her students identify similar concerns about the possible limitations of relying too much on students' knowledge: the standards for performance could be set too low by students as a result of laziness and/or ignorance; and the student-developed assessment developed by students might omit important elements unknown to the students.

Allison provides the remedy for these possible limitations in her discussion of the process she led, through which students developed a speech-making rubric. In this effort, Allison created a dialogue between her students' knowledge about speeches and a set of professional standards about effective speech making drawn from her curricular resources.

♦ Allison elicited ideas and insights from her students first: "Over the next few days we started making notes. I say *making* instead of *taking* because they (students) truly were constructing the notes....We began with content, then delivery, and finished with visual aids."

♦ She pointed out to herself and to her students the extent of their contribution to the rubric under construction: "We engaged in the same sort of note making for each speech component. I was astounded by how much these students knew! They were creating the notes themselves; I was merely the secretary who occasionally asked probing and/or clarifying questions."

♦ Allison enriched the rubric and assured its completeness by drawing on standards from relevant curricular resources: "I was working from a detailed model rubric another teacher had lent me so that I could make sure we covered the essential areas within each component."

Thus, Allison and her students enacted a dialogue that elicited and valued student knowledge and also incorporated necessary additional material from the professional knowledge base. The product of the dialogue was a rubric describing effective speech-making. The results were powerful, as Allison explains: "Unlike other times when I had given students notes on the very same information, students were fully engaged. They were discovering and processing the information in a much more meaningful way. Because they were creating the notes, the traditional 'checking for understanding' was built in, not tacked onto the lesson."

With practice Allison began to develop a pattern or template for the effective integration of these two elements, student knowledge and professional knowledge, in a way that encouraged both student engagement and high standards for the rubric. She explains:

> After a couple of speeches a pattern began to develop that seemed to work well. I began by providing the essential specifications of the speech assignment. For instance, when I assigned demonstration speeches, I began by telling students that the speech would have to demonstrate a process, be delivered with note cards, and be three to five minutes long. After I had provided these specifications, we devoted some class time to brainstorming possible topics and approaches that were appropriate to the assigned speech. For homework, students were assigned some beginning tasks such as selecting a topic and collecting source material. When we reconvened as a class, students were prepared to discuss the nuts and bolts of how the speeches would be assessed. This seemed like the right time to discuss the assessment tool; students had had the opportunity to discuss and work with the essential elements of the speech, and yet it was early enough in the speech process for the design of assessment to have a significant impact on students' work.

This is clearly an effective template for the integration of student knowledge and professional knowledge. What Allison might seek in her next steps is the application of the principles embedded in this template to the other key elements in her speech curriculum so that she can encourage the levels of student engagement that result from student-developed assessments. She might also incorporate appropriate elements from the professional literature into these assessment tools.

APPENDIX 1.1 — RUBRIC FORM

_____ Rubric

Name:_____ Date: _____

5	• • •	**DISTINGUISHED** Beyond New application Internalized
4	• • •	**PROFICIENT** Correct/clear Publishable No assistance needed
3	• • •	**CAPABLE** Nearly complete Revisable Needs assistance
2	• • •	**BEGINNER** Little shown work Fragmented Needs direction
1	• • •	**NOVICE** No/little order Missing elements Needs teaching
NS	Nonscoreable: No evidence or nothing turned in	

APPENDIX 1.2 — STUDENT QUESTIONNAIRE

NAME _____

For the purposes of this questionnaire, "student-developed assessments" are checklists, rubrics, grading criteria, and other methods of assessment developed by students for particular tasks (assignments) with teacher guidance. These assessments are then used by either or both the teacher and the student.

Please answer these questions as completely as possible.

1. Do you believe that assessments developed by students are valuable assessment tools? Explain.

2. Do you believe that student-developed assessments depict accurate student achievement? Explain.

3. Do student-developed assessments help students learn the material? Explain.

4. It takes a lot of class time to create student-developed assessments. Is the time spent worth it? Explain.

5. What experience in other classes have you had with student-developed assessment? Please be as specific as possible.

   Were these experiences positive or negative? Explain.

6. What are the advantages and disadvantages of student-developed assessment as compared to traditional teacher-developed assessment?

APPENDIX 1.3 — STUDENT SURVEY

Name (optional) _____

Please answer these questions as specifically as possible.

This semester we have used alternative forms of assessment for your speeches, often developed and assessed by you. You have not received individual letter or number grades on speeches; instead, you have been asked to review your taped speeches and reflect on your own growth and need for improvement. Please reflect on and explain the pros and cons of this approach *for your own learning.*

Pros   *Cons*

Would you have preferred teacher-developed and teacher-graded assessments?

If I were to use this approach again, what could be improved?

2

PROJECT ASSESSMENTS IN BLOCK PERIODS

Jeannie Wenndorf
Lindbergh High School

In her biology classes, Jeannie Wenndorf defined a *project assessment* as a student-developed project designed to evaluate the student's understanding of a given unit of study. She used such assessments instead of a traditional test at the end of some units. As a general rule, while the teacher provided the structure and the grading criteria for the project, the students provided the creativity and the content. The intent of a *project assessment* was to give students an opportunity to synthesize and apply major concepts they had learned in a unit.

Project assessments take time, so block periods are conducive to their use. Yet Wenndorf wondered whether the benefits to students of project assessments were sufficient given the time required?

Her data suggest that the answer is yes, because these assessments increase engagement in their learning for most students and encourage them both to solidify their previous learning and to expand upon it. In addition, these assessments involve students in developing teamwork skills. Wenndorf also identifies key reasons for the continued use of tests.

INTRODUCTION

I am a biology teacher at Lindbergh High School in Renton, Washington, a first-ring suburb of Seattle which includes both low and middle income neighborhoods. We serve approximately 1,220 students, grades 9–12, reflecting the following ethnic diversity: 17% Asian American, 10% African American, 3% Hispanic, 68% white, and 2% Native American Indian. I teach five sections of tenth grade biology, to be distinguished from the three sections of ninth grade honors biology also taught at Lindbergh. Thus, my population is primarily average students.

During my first three years at Lindbergh we followed the traditional high school schedule: six periods a day, fifty-five minutes each. In 1995, the staff at Lindbergh chose to move to block periods. Our current schedule looks like this:

First/fourth period:	7:20–9:04
Advisory:	9:09–9:34
Second/fifth period:	9:44–11:27
Lunch:	11:27–12:12
Third/sixth period:	12:17–2:00

Periods one, two, and three meet on Mondays and Thursdays, and periods four, five, and six meet on Tuesdays and Fridays. On Wednesdays, we revert to the traditional six-period day, which was our staff's compromise for those teachers who wish to see students at least three times a week, primarily the music and foreign language teachers.

DEVELOPMENT OF RESEARCH QUESTION

Three years ago, I piloted a biology curriculum that used alternative assessments as chapter evaluations. Though I often bemoaned the additional time and energy it took to prepare for and grade these assessments, I was intrigued by the opportunity they presented students to express what they had learned in creative ways. As I have grown as an educator, I have begun to modify these alternative assessments, creating what I call *project assessments* for my students. Block periods have been a catalyst for me in using project assessments, as the time structure lends itself to more creative, student-centered use of class time.

Let me begin by better defining *project assessment*. It is a student-developed project designed to evaluate the student's understanding of a given unit of study. It is administered instead of a traditional test, and its result is counted as a test grade. As a general rule, I provide the structure and the grading criteria for the project, while the students provide the creativity and the content. Typically, the students work in teams of two or four and present their final projects to the class for evaluation.

For example, I use a project assessment for a unit entitled "Disruption of Homeostasis." The unit focuses on how the human body responds to sickness or injury. At the end of this unit, students create a story about a person whose homeostasis has been disrupted. Their story must include reference to at least three disrupted organ systems, an explanation of the immune system's response, and a description of how the person's behavior influenced his or her risk for illness or injury, all content covered during the unit. Each team's story is then presented to the class in the form of a video, skit, puppet show, or storybook. The teacher, the presenters, and the audience of other students evaluate each story. The final score is considered a test grade; no other form of evaluation is given for this particular unit.

In contrast, in a unit on taxonomy, students do a weed-collection project. They are given a field guide to northwest weeds and go into the woods near the school to identify and collect weeds. Once collected, they mount their weeds on poster board and identify each by their common and scientific names. At the end of this unit, students take a traditional test on taxonomy. Though the weed collection is certainly a project, it is not an assessment. It is simply an activity within a unit that is designed to help students apply a given concept and some related skills (here, the science of identification and the use of scientific names).

So a project assessment is an activity that is given at the end of a particular unit of study, not somewhere in the middle. Its intent is to give students an opportunity to synthesize and apply the major concepts that they learned in a unit. It is used as an alternative to a traditional test.

Any teacher who has ever used them knows that project assessments tend to take more time than traditional tests. I have often wondered if that extra time is worthwhile. I have been willing to use class time for occasional project assessments because I perceive them to be more fun than traditional tests, for both students and myself, and thus more engaging for students. Hopefully this leads to a better learning experience and more effective content retention.

I decided to base my research question on these questions: Do students really like project assessments better than tests? Do they really retain information longer? If the answer to these questions is *yes*, then perhaps I am justified in continuing to use project assessments at the expense of covering more content. But if the answer is *no*, I may need to rethink how I use class time and how I evaluate student learning.

THE RESEARCH QUESTION

Are *project assessments* a valuable use of block periods in terms of student attitudes and content retention?

DATA COLLECTION PLAN

◆ To get a handle on how much additional time it really takes to use project assessments, I will look at old lesson plan books to determine how much class time is spent preparing for and administering traditional tests, in comparison with how much time is spent on project assessments.

◆ To answer the question of whether students prefer project assessments to traditional tests, I will have students complete two surveys. One will be specific to traditional tests and will be administered immediately following a traditional test. The other will be specific to project assessments and will be administered immediately following completion of a project assessment. (For survey questions and results, see Appendices 2.1, p. 47, and 2.2, p. 49.)

◆ To develop my understanding of student attitudes further, I will interview four students, including students of diverse ethnicity, gender, academic aptitude, and motivation. The interviews will be conducted after each student has completed both a traditional test and a project assessment, so that the distinction is clear. Questions will focus on students' attitudes toward each method of evaluation and their perception of content retention (see Appendix 2.3, p. 51).

◆ To measure retention, I will choose two classes to serve as test subjects. I will review each class' test averages so far this year and choose the two periods with the closest averages. After a specified unit, I will give one class a traditional test and the other a project assessment. Immediately following their respective evaluations, I will administer a short quiz that covers the main content of the unit, which will serve as a pretest for retention. A comparison of pretest scores will tell me whether either class learned more.

Approximately one month later, I will readminister the same quiz to both classes as a post-test. I will compare the post-test scores of each class to their pretest scores to determine how much information they retained. I will then compare the post-test scores of students who took the traditional test to the post-test scores of those who participated in the project assessment. This will give me information about whether either class retained more information than the other did.

◆ I will keep a journal in which I will record my reflections on the value of class time spent on the two evaluation methods, as well as students' enjoyment of and engagement in each method.

DATA ANALYSIS

Indeed, project assessments do take more time than traditional tests. However, I was surprised by the relatively small difference. According to my lesson plan book, project assessments required an average of only 40 minutes additional class time. In block periods, tests took an average of 83 minutes: typically 60 minutes to review and 20–30 minutes to administer. Project assessments averaged 120 minutes of class time: approximately 90 minutes of preparation and 30 minutes for presentations. This does not seem like an unreasonable difference. However, the particular project that was the focus of my research data showed a somewhat different comparison. For this project the classes that did project assessments needed 70 more minutes of class time than the class that took a traditional test.

On an interesting side note, old lesson plan books showed that project assessments in the 6-period day averaged a full 63 classroom minutes longer than they do in the block periods. This could mean that block periods lend themselves to more efficient student project work. Students are given a larger block of time in which to be creative and productive without interruption. It is also possible that I am getting better at planning and moderating efficient student projects. Most likely it is a combination of both.

The student surveys also indicate that projects took more time than tests. Students reported spending an average of 39 classroom minutes preparing for tests, with 61 of 98 students reporting less than 30 minutes. In contrast, students spent an average of 92 minutes of class time preparing for a project assessment, with only one of 105 students reporting less than 30 minutes spent. The results for nonclass-time preparation were similar: an average of 30 minutes was spent preparing for tests and 46 minutes was spent preparing for projects. Notably, 13 students reported spending more than 90 minutes outside of class working on their project, while only 4 students spent as much time preparing for a test.

The additional time needed for project assessments appears to be acceptable to students. When asked how much time was reasonable to spend preparing for a project assessment, the average response was 99 minutes, compared to only 57 minutes for test preparation. Fifty-seven students thought that more than 106 minutes was reasonable for project preparation; only 11 students said the same for tests.

However, not all students agreed that the additional time necessary to complete project assessments was worthwhile. Thirty-six students commented that tests are much quicker than projects. As one student put it, "I'd rather do a test. I mean they take too much time to do a project when a test only takes half an hour." Granted this comment reflects a misconception about how much time tests actually take, based on my data. It also reflects the attitude that less time spent on schoolwork is better, an attitude with which most teachers certainly disagree!

So is this additional class time worth it? Do students really like project assessments better? The results of student surveys on this matter are interesting. After completing a project assessment, 70% of students said they would prefer doing a project over a test. Yet when asked the very same question after taking a traditional test, only 49% of students said they would prefer a project to a test. Why this change of mind? I think students recognize that project assessments take more time and energy than tests. The fun and sense of accomplishment they experienced after presenting their projects made the extra effort seem worthwhile. But when they were surveyed again after taking a test for the next unit, many felt that it was quicker and easier just to take the test.

The comments of students who preferred project assessments seemed to fall into three general categories: projects are more fun than tests; you learn more doing a project; and working in groups is preferable to working alone. Let's explore each category in more detail.

PROJECTS ARE MORE FUN

Many students perceive project assessments to be less stressful than tests. They like the opportunity to be creative, as well as the change of pace from a traditional test. They see tests as boring and hard. One student boldly stated:

> I think tests are stupid; it's like the old times or something. People (teachers) should of thought of a better way to teach by now. I think projects are better because you know really probably only 10% of the students study [for tests]. But projects, you have to do them.

More students had positive feelings about projects than they did about tests. Thirty-seven percent of students liked or loved preparing their project. Only 18% liked or loved preparing for a test. Similarly, 42% of students reported that they liked or loved presenting their project; only 23% liked or loved taking a test. Notably, the 26 students (42%) who didn't like presenting their project attributed this to feeling uncomfortable speaking in front of the class.

YOU LEARN MORE DOING A PROJECT

Overall, 45% of students commented that projects make learning easier than tests. Some students learned more because they were having fun. One student wrote, "I loved the actual project. It made us think and research and have fun all at the same time. Good idea." Others attributed their learning to decreased stress. "Sometimes it is a lot harder to remember everything due to pressure [on a test] versus a project where you're writing and constantly talking about the lesson. I learned a lot more when we did projects."

Two of the students I interviewed credited their learning to the increased time spent with material. One said, "[Projects are] better for me because I spend more time on them. You have to get the grade. I don't have to study for a test. It's optional, since I can more or less guess on the test. I learn more with a project because I research it more."

The data from the pre-and post-tests support the assertion that students learn more with project assessments than tests. The class that participated in the project (the "project class") scored 4.9% higher on the pretest than the class that took the test (the "test class"). It is important to note, however, that on previous tests this school year, the project class averaged 1.7% higher test scores than the test class, which should be factored into these results. Similarly, on the post-test, the project class scored 5.1% higher than the test class. Thus, the project class students as a group, had a greater understanding of the content than did the test class students, to the extent of about a half grade, a month after the conclusion of the unit.

Perhaps project assessments encourage greater student learning because the project assessment is itself a learning experience. In the interviews I conducted, all four students clearly saw the purpose of tests as simply finding out what they had learned, whereas they thought that project assessments accomplished more than that. These assessments also develop team-building skills, teach new content, and encourage students to expand and share their knowledge of the unit.

Regardless of their reasons, students think project assessments are a more accurate measure of their learning than tests. Seventy-one percent of students noted that project assessments measure their learning pretty well to very well. Only 61% of students said the same about tests.

However, there is definitely a population of students who think they learn better with tests. As one student wrote, "I don't think I'll ever like taking a test, but I learn a lot more through tests than anything else." The test measures specific information and uses a wider range of the content taught in the unit. Students with good study skills learn a lot by reviewing class content, motivated by their desire to perform well on the test.

WORKING IN GROUPS IS PREFERABLE TO WORKING ALONE

The vast majority of students who prefer project assessments to tests mentioned group work as a key reason. Students like group work because it's fun and because there's an opportunity to share information and learn from each other. One student commented, "If you get stuck on something, you have the people in your group to help you out. Two brains are better than one." Another wrote, "I like to work with my team. Everybody in my team was helping each other when we needed them."

However, not all students had such a positive experience. Eleven percent of the students expressed frustration with their teammates. Most of their frustration stemmed from an unequal workload. One student explained, "My group didn't help, I did a lot of the work, and our grade suffered because of this. I would have liked it if the group work would have been more equal." Some students just plain prefer to work alone, especially when their grade is on the line. One student wrote, "I *hate* group activities which involve as many points as this one does. If someone's going to be in charge of my grade, I want it to be me, not the students in my group."

Entries from my reflection journal offer insight into the teacher's perspective. In my judgment, there is no question that student presentations are more fun than preparing for and taking tests for a considerable majority of students. In addition, most students are engaged more fully in their own process when they are creating, offering, and watching presentations. As I wrote in my journal, "The presentations were reasonably creative. Some of them were dull, others quite entertaining. I definitely had more fun watching their presentations than watching them take tests and then grading them....In conclusion, I like very much the final projects that were presented. It's more fun for me and the students, and they have much more invested in the project than in a test."

Whether preparing for project assessments is more fun for the teacher is another matter. It takes a lot more energy to manage a good project assessment than it does to give a good test. Some students need a lot of guidance on how to manage their time effectively on projects. After one particularly frustrating day, I wrote, "First and second periods gave me virtually no trouble today. Most kids were really trying and were productive. Third period, on the other hand, was a testy bunch. Few groups were consistently working. Most were chatting and would pretend to be working when I came around. I seriously doubt that the quality of their presentations will be very high. I'm afraid it will make me happy to give them poor grades for their final products....Projects are a lot of work for me. I get stressed out and tired." About tests I wrote, "Giving a test is easy. It takes very little preparation on my part, and very little work to monitor. Kids worked quietly in their seats while I graded papers at my desk."

In terms of student learning, I see value in both project assessments and tests. I think tests work well for developing individual accountability and study skills. But some students have such limited skills in these areas that they consistently do poorly on tests. They learn very little from tests because they simply don't study.

Project assessments, on the other hand, engage the students more in the learning process and encourage more higher-level thinking. Project assessments also give students more of an opportunity to synthesize and apply the knowledge they've gained. But in reality, I was somewhat disappointed with the quality of the students' projects. "Most kids did a decent job presenting the additional information they'd uncovered, and not so decent a job of applying their topic to the [chapter content]. That was frustrating, as that was the whole point of the project. However, when I consider the alternative (testing), I'm sure I would have gotten similar results." Also, because higher-level thinking is hard, students tend to become frustrated and quit trying. One day, I wrote, "It's so frustrating to me to watch kids piddle away their time when I know the end result is going to be a failing grade on their project. Lots of them just don't seem to make the connection, or don't seem to care. I hate it when I care more about their learning than they do."

A related issue involves assigning the same grade to each member of a project team. I raised an interesting point in my journal: "I did get the feeling that the quality of the presentation's content was directly proportional to the smartest kid on the team. Is this bad? I don't know. Yes, the other kids on the team benefited from the smartest kids' understanding of the subject matter, but isn't that the point of working in teams? That way the less intelligent kids are more likely to 'get it' by the conclusion of the project, where they never would have if I just tested them. However, this did skew the grades a bit on the high side." A student echoed my concern in the survey: "[A test] shows what you know. On a project it shows what the smartest person in your group knows."

Clearly there are pros and cons to project assessments. But what about retention: Did students retain any more information because of the project? When asked how long they thought they would remember the information on which they were just evaluated, 51% of students said "one year" or "forever" after taking a test. Fifty-eight percent said the same after completing a project assessment. So there is some perception among students that they remember information longer with a project.

The data from the pre- and post-tests do indicate that students remember more after completing a project assessment, but the difference is minimal. The test class' post-test scores were 3.7% lower than their pretest scores, while the project class scores dropped by 3.5% This does not suggest a significant difference in retention rate.

ACTION PLAN

As I review my research, I find many reasons to support continued use of project assessments. They don't take an excessive amount of additional class time, and they provide an alternative to a traditional test. Students like project assessments because they are fun and allow students to work together and be creative. The evidence that project assessments increase student learning is a powerful motivator for me. And even if they don't significantly increase students' retention, at least they don't lower retention, so what's the harm?

However, because of the teacher energy it takes to manage project assessments effectively, I do not foresee project assessments replacing tests. The last paragraph in my reflection journal reads, "Now that it's over, I do think [completing project assessments] was a worthwhile experience. I'm not willing to do this every time, but perhaps once a quarter is reasonable. I think you have to do project assessments more than once to teach the kids how to do a good job with it. It takes everyone some time to get the hang of it and learn to use their time efficiently. But I do have to say I'm glad it's over. I'm exhausted."

The next logical step for me is to explore how to make the next project assessment better. "I'm learning that to make a project successful, it has to be a well-designed project. The directions need to be clear, so kids know what to do. The kids have to know the content from class, so they can effectively include it in their project. There has to be available information for kids, so that they don't get frustrated with pointless research. There have to be appropriate time frames to work in, and appropriate/immediate consequences to motivate kids to use time efficiently."

How can class time be used more efficiently? This particular project assessment involved student research in the library. This activity proved to be frustrating for me, as I discovered that students have not necessarily been taught how to research. Much of the time I allotted for project preparation was fruitless, as students were unable to come up with any useful information. Next time I will try assigning the research stage of the project as homework. Students will have one week to gather information using the library, Internet, or other resources. Class time can then be dedicated to sharing and applying student research and to developing presentations.

How can I encourage students to be better team members and distribute the workload equitably? I got the feeling from a lot of students that the reason they prefer project assessments to tests is because they can do relatively little work and still get a good grade by "piggybacking" the smart people in their group. If I can solve this problem, perhaps project assessments will be a better experience for those students who were frustrated by less than helpful team members.

I tried to encourage individual accountability by giving each team a large chunk of points, equivalent to the score they'd earned on the project multiplied by the number of people on their team. They could then distribute those points among their team however they saw fit. This helped some, but a lot of students felt uncomfortable taking points away from their friends. Perhaps next time I will allow students to choose their own teams. My guess is that the students who don't want to work hard will choose each other; then at least their lack of effort won't negatively impact others. Ideally, this will force the lesser-motivated kids to work harder because there will be no one else to do the work for them.

Student comments cause me to wonder how I can do a better job with traditional tests. I need to work on making the process of reviewing for tests more fun. Occasionally, I'll play a review game with students, but usually I just give them a set of review questions to guide their studying. I think students would appreciate it if I put a little more effort and creativity into test reviews.

I'd also like to explore how tests themselves could be made more engaging and meaningful. Because they're so easy to grade, I tend to use multiple choice tests, with a few short-answer questions at the end. Yet the students I interviewed did not see multiple choice tests as the best tool for evaluating a student's knowledge. They would rather have the opportunity to explain the information in their own words than to choose from a list of teacher-generated responses, although they readily admit that multiple choice tests are easier. I'd like to add more variety to my test repertoire in response to this feedback. Project assessments are a step in the right direction.

Finally, I'd like to learn more about what helps students remember content. My data did not show that project assessments or tests were particularly influential in retention rates. In my interviews, when I asked students about this ("What do you think really influences how much you will remember from a class?"), not one student mentioned tests or projects, even though they knew that was the focus of my project. They consistently mentioned meaningful, interesting, and fun activities. I would like to learn more about which activities students perceive to be meaningful, interesting and fun, and whether these activities really affect content retention.

In conclusion, it seems my choice to use project assessments, as well as tests, as evaluation tools is warranted. Gathering data to back up my assumptions was an important step in making solid educational decisions. I felt like a true partner with my students in seeking to understand the value of various assessment strategies. This research has helped me see more clearly what I do well, and how I can do a better job developing meaningful, engaging assessment tools in the years to come.

IDEAS FOR NEXT STEPS

In this study, Jeannie Wenndorf explored the uses of project assessments in her biology classes. In her construction of such assessments, Wenndorf provided "the structure and the grading criteria for the project, the students provide[d] the creativity and the content." While this approach has its value, a next step that Wenndorf might consider is the adoption of Kimberly Allison's model for student-developed assessment. While involving students in the development of their own project rubric would require class time for instruction about rubric qualities, such an innovation would likely produce results similar to those described by Allison in terms of increased student understanding of what constitutes a good project and why. It might also help to increase student motivation and raise her students' own standards in relation to the quality of their project assessment work.

Another step for Wenndorf to consider is the articulation of projects that include both individual and group accountability. Such an approach would remedy the problem she describes in which some students seem to coast on the work of others. In addition she may want to provide her students with some specific instruction about effective teamwork roles and skills. While this may seem to distract from her biology focus, even a minimum of teaching about how to work together effectively could provide long-term benefits to her students' learning.

APPENDIX 2.1 — STUDENT SURVEY: TRADITIONAL EXAM

Please consider your experience with the test you just completed when answering the following questions. Circle your response to each question. Please feel free to make additional comments if desired.

[Results are shown in bold print.]

1. How much class time (in minutes) did you spend preparing for the test (i.e., studying, working on review questions)?

0	1-15	16-30	31-45	46-60	61-75	76-90	91-105	106+
5	32	24	12	8	6	2	2	7

2. How much nonclass time (in minutes) did you spend preparing for the test (i.e., studying, working on review questions)?

0	1-15	16-30	31-45	46-60	61-75	76-90	91-105	106+
20	26	2	7	9	3	0	3	1

3. How much total time (in minutes) do you think is reasonable to spend preparing for a test?

0	1-15	16-30	31-45	46-60	61-75	76-90	91-105	106+
3	8	13	18	24	10	5	2	11

4. Did you like preparing for this test?

1	2	3	4	5
hated it	didn't like it	it was ok	liked it	loved it
9	15	53	14	3

Why?

5. Did you like taking this test?

1	2	3	4	5
hated it	didn't like it	it was ok	liked it	loved it
10	19	47	18	5

Why?

6. How accurately did this test measure your learning?

1	2	3	4	5
not at all	a little	some	pretty well	very well
2	10	26	49	12

7. If you had your choice, how would you prefer to have your learning evaluated? (Circle one.)

multiple choice test	project
50	48

List three things you like about that particular method.
1.
2.
3.

8. How long do you think you'll remember the information you were just tested on?

5 minutes	1 week	1 month	3-6 months	1 year	forever
2	15	11	16	17	36

9. Additional comments you'd like to make about tests:

APPENDIX 2.2 — STUDENT SURVEY: PROJECT ASSESSMENT

Please consider your experience with the project assessment you just completed when answering the following questions. Circle your response to each question. Please feel free to make additional comments if desired.

> **Definition of "project assessment":** a project, developed and presented by the student, designed to evaluate the student's understanding of a given unit of study; administered instead of a traditional test and counted as a test grade.

[Results are shown in bold print.]

1. How much class time (in minutes) did you spend working on the project assessment (i.e., researching, planning with team, practicing for presentation, etc.)?

0	1-15	16-30	31-45	46-60	61-75	76-90	91-105	106+
0	**0**	**1**	**8**	**9**	**5**	**23**	**17**	**42**

2. How much nonclass time (in minutes) did you spend working on the project assessment?

0	1-15	16-30	31-45	46-60	61-75	76-90	91-105	106+
7	**16**	**24**	**12**	**5**	**6**	**5**	**3**	**10**

3. How much total time (in minutes) do you think is reasonable to spend working on a project assessment?

0	1-15	16-30	31-45	46-60	61-75	76-90	91-105	106+
0	**1**	**0**	**0**	**3**	**8**	**14**	**21**	**57**

4. Did you like working on this project?

1	2	3	4	5
hated it	didn't like it	it was ok	liked it	loved it
4	**11**	**52**	**27**	**13**

Why?

5. Did you like presenting your project to the class?

1	2	3	4	5
hated it	didn't like it	it was ok	liked it	loved it
1	**11**	**50**	**39**	**6**

Why?

6. How accurately did your project/presentation measure your learning?

1	2	3	4	5
not at all	a little	some	pretty well	very well
1	**7**	**22**	**61**	**12**

7. If you had your choice, how would you prefer to have your learning evaluated? (Circle one.)

multiple choice test	project
31	**71**

List three things you like about that particular method.
1.
2.
3.

8. How long do you think you'll remember the information included in your project?

5 minutes	1 week	1 month	3-6 months	1 year	forever
4	**7**	**21**	**12**	**12**	**50**

8. Additional comments you'd like to make about project assessments:

APPENDIX 2.3 — STUDENT INTERVIEW QUESTIONS

Student Name ⎯⎯⎯⎯⎯⎯⎯⎯⎯⎯⎯⎯

1. What do you see as the purpose of tests?

2. Do you think tests really accomplish that purpose for you? Why or why not?

3. How much class time do you think should be spent preparing for tests? Taking tests?

4. What is your general attitude toward tests?

5. What do you see as the purpose of project assessments?

6. Do you think projects really accomplish that purpose for you? Why or why not?

7. How much class time do you think should be spent preparing for projects? Presenting projects?

8. What is your general attitude toward project assessments?

9. What do you think really influences how much you will remember from a class?

10. What advice would you give a teacher about accurately evaluating what you have learned?

11. Anything else you'd like to say about how you are and/or would like to be evaluated?

3

STUDENT INITIATIVE AND RESPONSIBILITY IN USING *PROJECT TIMES* IN BLOCK PERIODS

Mark Lovre
Cedarcrest High School

In his junior and senior English classes, Mark Lovre created a structure in which he conducted teacher-led activities for part of each block period and gave students *project time*, varying from 20 to 80 minutes, to work on a set of projects for which they were responsible. Projects included an array of writing assignments, speeches, debates, presentations, and so on.

Could his students learn to manage their own in-class time use effectively enough to make its daily availability worthwhile? Could they learn to work on several projects simultaneously for this one class? And if so, how much teacher direction would they need to help them accomplish this task?

What Lovre learns is that almost all of his students value the opportunities he gives them for enhanced responsibility and initiative and that many of his students can take significant steps toward greater responsibility and more effective time management, although movement in these directions is inconsistent for some students. As students become more able to use their in-class time well, they become more engaged with the activities of the class.

Lovre also learns that he needs to develop further his own teaching skills in organizing his classroom and curriculum toward these ends.

RESEARCH QUESTIONS

To what extent do students use *project time* effectively? How can I improve the quality of their use of this time?

Project time is time in class when students are expected to work on various projects, which have due dates from one week to eight weeks from the date of assignment. I assign three or four projects within each literature unit along with one long-term paper, which includes several interim assignments and due dates.

INTRODUCTION

Cedarcrest High School in Duvall, Washington, has been on an extended block period schedule since it opened in the fall of 1993. Duvall is a small town 30 miles east of Seattle, and the school includes small town, rural, and growing suburban and exurban populations. The "Cedarcrest Plan" called for a three-period day. Each student would be enrolled only in three 100-minute classes at a time. The school year is split into four nine-week terms, with each teacher having a 100-minute preparation period for half of the year. Thus, each teacher still taught the equivalent of five classes, the norm in the six-period day schedule. Most departments' courses are 18 weeks long. English courses are nine weeks long. For example, juniors take nine weeks of writing II and nine weeks of American literature.

Near the end of the third term I began focusing on the questions for this action research project: to what extent do students use *project time* effectively, and how can I help them to become more effective in their use of this time? I wanted to address the issue of the effective use of time by my students,

55

and I also wanted to reflect on my class system as a whole. Is it worthwhile? Does it help students to learn? To begin the research, I started an informal contemporaneous journal on the topic, and I asked my eleventh and twelfth graders to write thoughtfully about how the structure of their respective courses affected their learning in terms of content, time-management, and responsibility. These comments, the discussions they sparked, and my own reflections led to the development of the research questions, their analysis, and some conclusions about the future of my classroom system.

CLASSROOM SYSTEM

I began teaching at Cedarcrest in the 1995–96 school year. I taught mostly junior and senior level literature courses and some junior writing. My style, like most first-year teachers, was one of survival. I received a lot of valuable assistance from my fellow English teachers in terms of techniques and content, and the year went well. My survival instincts during this year helped me develop a classroom management approach based on a personable, informal style. I founded my management, and therefore much of my teaching, on a casual classroom atmosphere with open discussions about course content and a willingness to explore related topics that arose from student interests. I did my best to steer the discussions toward English-related topics, but decided early on that if I could keep the students involved and thinking, I could allow the subjects of our discussions to expand beyond the formal curriculum. I also tended to give the students a few projects at a time so that I could buy time for myself to catch up or to keep my head above water.

Over the summer I decided that I would take my survival instincts and turn them into a meaningful system for running my classes. This year, I have been implementing and tinkering with this system. In a nine-week junior literature course, there are four units, each based on one primary work of fiction and including additional fiction and nonfiction readings (we don't use English textbooks in the upper grades at Cedarcrest). Each of these units has three to five projects, which are assigned at the beginning of the unit and are due at the end of the unit. These projects are one- to three-week assignments that allow the students to show that they have an understanding of the readings and class discussions over the course of the unit. There are a wide variety of projects, and they are done in groups, pairs, and individually. The range of projects includes critical essays, creative writing, performance of skits, speeches, debates, collages, board games, and peer teaching. In addition to the unit projects, my literature courses assign an overarching, eight-week author paper for which the student must read an author's work, research the author's life, and write a five-page paper. Each project requires a specific sets of skills and is evaluated with a rubric. In addition to the projects that go with each unit, class time is spent on vocabulary, reading quizzes, discussion, reading aloud, exams, and lessons and activities that introduce or reinforce the skills on which the class is working. (In this study, *class time* refers to time in class during which the teacher directly leads activities. *Project time* refers to time in class during which students work on their projects, without direct teacher control.)

One hundred-minute periods allow this system to work. On every class day, there are 20 to 80 minutes available for *project time*. During this time the students can work on whatever they choose for my class. At any time, a student has four or five projects to work on and two books to read. In *project time*, I circulate through the class (and the hall and library) for individual coaching, questions, guidance, and minilessons. I recall all of the students to the class to address widespread needs as they arise.

This system places responsibility for organization and time management on the students' shoulders. From the very beginning of the course, I discuss responsibility, time management, and procrastination. I tell the students that I will not constantly remind them to be on task, and that it is up to them to make the connections between effective use of time, learning, and successful grades. My goal is to avoid badgering the students; I want them to make the connections for themselves. The extended block periods give me the flexibility to do traditional English class activities and still have time to set up the students to be responsible for dealing with multiple tasks over time.

In terms of the research questions, *effective* for this classroom system means that most or all of the students are on task most or all of the time. *Effective* also includes these elements:

- making well-considered decisions about time management
- making connections between units
- asking appropriate questions
- applying what students have learned previously to the tasks at hand
- helping each other to succeed
- using all the available resources to complete their projects to a standard of accomplishment.

This system is still very much in progress, and it has changed every term of the year. The system works best with my personality and style of running a class and interacting with students. It allows me to know my students better and to track their problems effectively. Because Cedarcrest uses an inclusion model, this system also allows me to teach IEP (individual education plan) students more effectively, with more one-on-one time, more time to interact with educational assistants, and more time to monitor IEP students' progress and all students' learning. The effective implementation of this system would balance reminders from me to be on task with the need for the students to make their own connections between their use of time and their learning and achievement in the class.

TERM FOUR: AMERICAN LITERATURE CLASSES

After spending nearly three terms this year working with this system, I began, through personal reflection, to look more carefully at what was effective about its elements and what was not, adjusting what I did in the classroom, and having discussions with my students. For my initial formal gathering of data, I asked my term three students to write a one-page response to the prompt: "How has the structure of this course affected your learning in terms of both subject content and skills?" We discussed the meaning of the prompt and came to understand "subject content" as traditional English class items such as reading, writing, literature, and so on. We interpreted "skills" to mean other capacities and topics raised by the system, such as time management, organization, and issues regarding procrastination. We talked about focusing students' writing on one or two specific areas instead of trying to cover everything in one page. I also reminded students that I would not read their comments until they were gone and their grades were turned in, so that they could be honest without fear of reprisal. They took the assignment seriously, although about half of the 60 papers ended up being quite general.

The messages in these papers covered a wide spectrum of issues. Students had both praise and criticism for the class structure. Many praised the laid-back atmosphere. Many criticized the stress of the class. Several did both in the same paper. Several common themes emerged from the comments. The primary positive aspect of the system was the freedom involved. Students consistently commented on feeling responsible and not having to sit still for endless minutes. One student wrote, "The freedom to work at our own pace also encouraged freedom of thought. Discussions emerged which allowed us to form our own conclusions." Students also commented positively about issues of time management and procrastination. One senior explained, "At first, I took advantage of the time to socialize, then I would have so much homework that I would be stressed out. I gradually realized that all off this free time could be used for discussion and it was teaching me time management." The main negative comments about the class were a desire for more teacher-initiated discussions, the desire for more reminders of due dates, and a decrease in the amount of group work.

My interpretation of these responses, coupled with my reflections on term three in general, led me to begin term four a little differently. I didn't want to undermine the students' ability to make connections between use of time and achievement by constantly badgering them in class, but it was obvious that a clearer, more in-depth explanation of the system was needed at the beginning of each new class. To this end, I rewrote my syllabi and spent much more time explaining the notion of *project time* in the first few days of the term. I explained the need for time management and keeping track of several assignments at a time. I also clarified my expectations for the first set of projects, which were assigned in the first week of class for the first unit, the Puritans. We had several discussions in the first week about what it meant to be on task and about asking questions for clarification of either assignments or the material. We also talked about the need for students not to wait for me to guide them at every turn. Thus, responding to the student feedback from term three, I had made the fundamental ideas of my system clearer than they had been before, to both my students and myself.

The Puritan unit centered on *The Crucible* and went well. Students were generally on task during both class time and *project time*. We also began the author paper assignment at this time. This five-page paper required students to choose an American author, read one or two of her or his works (depending on their length and degree of challenge), research the author's life and work, and write a thesis to drive their paper. The paper could be either a research effort or a piece of literary criticism. This paper had five interim due dates and one final due date, all of which were in the last four weeks of the term. We discussed the need for students to read consistently both during *project time* and during their homework time. I suggested some note-taking and research strategies for balancing the reading of two different books at the same time. (The book for their author paper and the book we were reading together for class.) In trying to balance reminders to students about their need to stay on top of the workload with a desire not to badger them, I used discussions at the beginning of class once a week to talk about work habits and strategies for reading and writing independently. The projects for the Puritan unit were good; no one failed to meet minimum requirements.

The next unit was the weakest of the term. In retrospect, I had not made the expectations as clear as they should have been, and the projects for the one and a half weeks unit were not well written. The students were reading Jefferson, Franklin, Washington, Emerson, Thoreau, Whitman, Lincoln, and

Poe. Much of the material was very difficult for them to understand, and I tried to cover it in too short a time, both by asking students to read too much and by providing them with inadequate background and support. During the unit, the students' frustration levels rose, and they lost focus both during class time and *project time*. As a result of this loss of focus during *project time*, they were also falling behind on their author paper reading.

At the end of this unit, we debriefed our experience from this week and a half, vented some frustrations, and discussed ways to improve the curriculum expectations and activities. In addition to their criticism about the amount of difficult reading assigned in a short time, students noted that their projects—making a presentation about one piece of writing with a poster board aid and writing a short critical essay—were due before they'd had adequate time to understand the material. I felt that we did a good job of constructively criticizing the problems, and students began the next unit, *Huckleberry Finn*, with open minds. There were four projects in this unit, as well as the ongoing author paper and day-to-day class activities.

During this unit, the first author paper due dates came up. We were very busy in the class, and the students began to be overwhelmed. I used this as an opportunity to discuss time management and student responsibility issues once again. The discussions seemed to go well, but the students were not implementing their ideas effectively. Off-task behavior was more noticeable and frustration levels were higher than they had been before. Although they were understanding the novel, they were not using their *project time* well.

A couple of issues surfaced in my observations at this time. First, I concluded that the students had not been reading steadily on their author paper books, so they were forced to cram for the first due dates for these papers. I also noticed that one class was not multitasking effectively. Most of the students in the class were waiting until one project was done or nearly done before they began the next one. With all projects due within a two-day span, this was not a way to ensure success.

As we completed the novel and the projects, we had some short discussions about students' performance and their feelings of frustration. We talked about ways to deal with the amount of work and more effective self-monitoring of students' use of time in the classroom. Several students indicated that they wanted more reminders of due dates and especially a more controlling teacher presence in the classroom during *project time*. This led others to respond by commenting that more reminders would undermine the purposes of setting up the class system in this way. There was some very thoughtful dialogue among the students about the very issues I was trying to work with in this system—individual responsibility and time management—and whether or not these qualities and skills were being learned. I was pleased that some students were making the connection between their success, or lack thereof, in effectively balancing several projects at once with their learning of the concepts, qualities, and skills of personal efficacy that I was seeking to infuse into my curriculum.

SURVEY

Toward the middle of the *Huckleberry Finn* unit I gave students a survey about the classroom system, which we had already implemented, for almost a month, through two plus units. The survey had eight questions, five of which had a numeric scale attached (see Appendix 3.1, p. 71). The questions covered a range of issues, from how well students felt they had used their *project time* to their perceptions of the strengths and weaknesses of the classroom system. Before I gave the survey to students, we developed a list of the various aspects of the system and its goals on the board and clarified some vocabulary found in the survey. I assured the students that these surveys would not affect their grades or my relationships with them, either for better or worse. I told them that I wanted honest responses that neither kissed up to me nor brutalized me. I gave them the survey, had them read through it, and had them ask any questions about it. I believe they felt comfortable with the survey, and their responses seemed genuine.

The first survey question was: "Were the purposes of this system made clear to you?" The responses indicated that I had done a good-to-excellent job of laying out the system clearly in the beginning (66% of the students ranked this a 5 or a 4 on a 5-point scale, with 5 meaning "very clear"). The comments revealed that I should have revisited the subject of the classroom system more often and more directly during the opening weeks of the term. One student wrote, "I was told at the beginning of the term exactly how the system was to be run." However, another explained, "It was never explained to us until this survey was brought up." The majority of comments indicated a progression: "At first I was a little unclear, but now I have the swing of things and I understand how to make good use of my class time." The responses told me that I should initiate more student-driven discussions about the system as we work on the first units. Perhaps working to get students to draw and state the conclusions for themselves about what they need to do to be successful within this classroom system will be more effective at conveying these insights earlier in the term.

The second question was: "Do you prioritize (or work on several) tasks in class? How does this affect your success?" Eighty-six percent of the students indicated a 4 or a 3 on a 5-point scale, with 5 meaning "always" and 3 meaning "sometimes." The comments demonstrated that this was a set of skills on which students needed to improve. One student wrote, "When I actually do prioritize my tasks, I find a lot more success. I am getting better at it since it is so important in this class." This student noted that he prioritized tasks sometimes, and that he recognized this pattern as one in which he could improve. Another student wrote, "I usually work on whatever's due first. This usually works out, but sometimes I don't leave myself enough time to work on something." Finally, a student wrote, "If prioritizing wasn't done, it would be impossible to pass the class."

Students wrote about the importance of prioritizing tasks and working on more than one assignment at a time, but they indicated that they didn't do this consistently. What I've learned from this is that I need to teach multitasking and prioritizing skills directly. I see now that I have asked some students to perform in ways for which they do not yet have the necessary skills. For next year I will explore this issue further and will likely work with students directly on the skills and tools for personal management, including course organizers, calendars, journals, breaking down large projects into manageable tasks, and keeping track of works in progress.

The third survey question asked students how effectively they used *project time* during class. Again, the numeric responses were primarily in the 4 and 3 range on a 5-point scale, with 5 meaning "very well." The comments ranged from "I use my time very well" to "Mostly, I yap with others." Another student wrote, "It is hard for me to be able to work effectively inside your class with the people who don't use class time to its full purpose." The need for multiple work areas, and especially a designated quiet area, came through clearly in the responses to this question.

The survey's fourth question continued the same line of inquiry: "How strong is the connection between your use of time in class and your learning?" On a 5-point scale, with 5 meaning "very strong," 51% of the students circled 4, and 26% circled 3. Comments ranged from "The time I use in class gives me an opportunity to retain the information that I'm being taught" to "I could use my time a little better and learn a little more." A few students wrote along these lines: "I feel that I learn very little in this or any other English class I have taken that involves reading as a large portion of class." The majority of students seemed to understand the connection between their use of time and their learning, but I don't believe that the same number were able to act on that understanding consistently.

I walk a careful line on the issue of students using time in class effectively. It is very important to me for students to make connections between their use of *project time* and their learning and academic success in my class. I feel that the more I harp on their need to be responsible, the less I am letting them make those connections. Nonetheless I need to improve in this aspect of my teaching by discussing this issue more often during the opening portion of the term. I've also become aware of an intriguing complexity in this teaching equation: To some important extent I need to allow students to try and fail in their efforts at personal management, because a good number of students seem to learn best from experiencing the consequences of their own failure and then making needed corrections. My role in this transaction must be to support their efforts to learn by simultaneously assisting them and holding them responsible within a nonpunitive interpersonal atmosphere.

The fifth survey question asked the students to rate the usefulness of this system for their learning of course content. In the discussions prior to completing the survey, we had agreed that course content meant the usual skills one thought of when dealing with an English class (reading comprehension, writing, vocabulary, grammar, and critical thinking) as well as the literature itself. I was surprised by the numerical data on this one: 71% of the students marked a 4 or a 5, with 5 meaning "very useful." One student wrote, "This system is great in the way that it forces you to be independent and rely on yourself (much of which is like how next year and college will be like)." Another said, "I feel I learn more in most areas of this class because it is up to me to pay attention and it is up to me to ask questions when I don't understand. This makes me feel like what I am learning is not being forced upon me." In contrast, one student wrote, "We should do one thing at a time but do them quicker." Another wrote simply, "We need to go over stuff more."

I believe that in many ways this system encourages enhancement of student English skills, which they have already developed to some extent, because they practice and further develop their skills in all the group contexts. The tutoring and minilessons that I provide during *project time* further support students' skills. However, for skills that are new to students, a structured, teacher-centered program of instruction is more effective. I need to examine this issue more carefully when I consider the ratio in my class between *project time* and class time.

The sixth question on the survey asked if the system had taught students about the use of time and the nature of personal responsibility. This was a weak question in that its intent had already been covered in previous questions. However, the comments did cover a range, from "This system definitely helped me work on my procrastination problem" to "No, I figured out how to manage my time and get stuff done a long time ago."

The last two survey questions were open-ended and asked about the strengths of the system and how it could be improved. The strengths listed were unsurprising: students noted the openness, the similarity to their vision of what college would be like, the fact that it forced them to be organized and responsible, and that they enjoyed the independence in the class. Several students mentioned the pacing and the ability of students and teacher to establish better relationships in the class. One student wrote that one quality of the teacher's role he liked was "the not being a mommy part."

The aspects of the system which students listed for improvement included shifting the time spent on regular class items and *project time* (interestingly enough, about as many students wanted more *project time* as wanted less), addressing procrastination more directly, eliminating the author paper, and having more teacher-centered lessons on English content. Many students wanted some adjustments of due dates. Others wanted due dates recorded on the board. Many also wished that the due dates for each unit's projects were not grouped so closely together. They wanted a more linear, one-project-at-a-time system for the class.

LAST UNIT AND INTERVIEWS

In the last four weeks of the term, we finished the *Huckleberry Finn* projects and debriefed the experience as it related both to the content of the unit and to the class system. We had one unit left, plus the bulk of the writing, revising, and editing of the author papers. We began *The Great Gatsby* and the four projects that went with it, and we started focusing some class lessons on the composition of the author paper. The students seemed to be using their time pretty well. I suspected that many of the students were trying to catch up, or cover up, regarding the work they had not yet done for their author papers. Students commented that they were enjoying the novel, and that they found it easier to understand than *Huckleberry Finn*. As the end of the term approached, however, things started to drift. The end of the year was nearing, and students were trying to rush me through the regular class-time portions of the period, so they could get into project work. At the same time, the students were progressing well on their *Gatsby* projects, and we discussed the lessons they had learned about focus and time management over the course of the term.

While their *Gatsby* projects were going well, I began to work with them on their author papers more directly, and I discovered where many students had gotten the time to do well with *The Great Gatsby*. The process of writing the papers was barely begun for a lot of these students. I was shocked. The writing of a five-page thesis paper was not new to any of them, and yet many students were unprepared to do good work and were scrambling to find a way to get by at the last minute. As it was the end of the term and the year, I felt I had no choice but to adjust the schedule and go back to square one with the papers. We discussed the problems at length, and there were no good excuses from the students nor from me. I had let a major assignment progress to the final weeks without realizing how badly off many of my students were.

Because it was the end of the year, I felt that I had to adjust my plans. While I communicated my disappointment to my students, to simply give them the poor grades they would have earned did not feel fair. Perhaps it would have been an effective lesson in responsibility at another point in the year. Now I wanted to give them additional opportunities to complete their work. The *Gatsby* projects went well, and the students used their time more effectively than they had at any point during the term. Nonetheless, the author papers, even with more time available, were a struggle for students, who produced mostly mediocre work.

In the final days of the term, I conducted several interviews with students that I based on the week four survey. I found that the students interviewed reflected views similar to those on the surveys. They recognized the value of focusing on time management and on individual responsibility but also wanted more teacher guidance, reminders, and specific skills taught about how to be successful in the system. Different students had different wishes, but all except one basically liked the system and thought that it was worth keeping. Hindsight had lessened the stress on these students, and their comments were less intense than they had been earlier in the term. All characterized the system, to some extent, as being "as close to the real world as English class will ever get."

Conclusions

My primary conclusion is that this system is worthwhile, and it deserves the time and attention it needs to become truly effective. The system allows for the learning and practice of English content skills (reading, writing, thinking, and literature) while pushing the students to think consciously about time management and responsibility issues. Most of my students used their *project time* fairly well, and all of them were aware by term four that the use of time was important both to learning and to academic success in the class. This system allows for more one-on-one time for the teacher with individual students, and it allows me to get to know students better in terms of their learning styles, skill levels, and progress. This is especially valuable because Cedarcrest uses the inclusion model for special-needs students. This system allows me to work more personally with IEP students and with the educational assistants to tailor clear and meaningful programs for them.

There are clearly many ways that I can improve the system. My primary focus will be on assessment. I need to clarify the objectives for each project in each unit and tie these together more effectively across the entire course. This clarification will allow me to use these objectives to create clear and meaningful rubrics for all of the projects. Better rubrics will allow the students to work more meaningfully and learn better. The clarification of my objectives will also allow me to work with the development of skills across 9- or 18-week blocks of time. Unit planning and course planning are the two key areas for improving the system next year.

To improve the development of time management skills within each unit, I will introduce interim due dates and checkups to make sure students are working on all of the projects in a given unit. Many students made it clear that they were waiting until one project was due, or nearly due, before they began the next project. Because all of the projects are due within a two- or three-day period, this weakened both the work they produced for the second and subsequent projects and the learning that went on through their completion. In addition to interim due dates, I will spend more time at the beginning of the course teaching organizational and time-management skills. I will introduce course organizers as well as note-taking and short- and long-term organization techniques, and reinforce these concepts and skills throughout the course.

I will also reassess the workload over the whole course. All English courses are moving from 9 weeks to 18 weeks next year, so the amount of work per curriculum unit over the course of the term will be as important as the alignment of content and skills objectives for the course. This is especially important because next year basic classes will be added at every grade level. These classes are to cover the same basic content but are to go more slowly and focus on fundamental skills and basic understanding. It will be critical to modify this system for it to work well for that population. The system has been a boon for the IEP students in the inclusion model, but I must approach a basic course carefully, particularly in terms of the amount of free time I allow and how it is used. It became clear this term that some of the units seemed harder than others, and the rhythm of the work didn't always seem smooth. As I work on the alignment of skills over the 18-week course, I will work on the amount and type of work I am asking of the students as well. I can analyze tasks in terms of the time and the energy required of the students for success, to eliminate inconsistencies within the system. Also, next year I will finish integrating the six-trait writing model into my classes, so I will be working to effectively teach and reinforce that model in the context of the *project time* system.

IDEAS FOR NEXT STEPS

In this study, Mark Lovre examined the effectiveness of his classroom system in relation to his students' abilities to manage multiple assignments and the effective use of *project time.* At the end of his study, Lovre identified his own next steps with clarity and insight. First, he wrote,

> I need to clarify the objectives for each project in each unit and tie these together more effectively across the entire course. This clarification will allow me to use these objectives to create clear and meaningful rubrics for all of the projects. Better rubrics will allow the students to work more meaningfully and learn better. The clarification of my objectives will also allow me to work with the development of skills across 9- or 18-week blocks of time.

Once he has developed several project rubrics himself and used them with students, Lovre might consider involving his students in the collaborative development of project rubrics.

Next Lovre identified changes in the structure of assignments that he plans to introduce:

> To improve the development of time management skills within each unit, I will introduce interim due dates and checkups to make sure students are working on all of the projects in a given unit.

Finally, Lovre described additional skills that he needs to teach directly to his students so that they are likely to be more successful within the classroom system he has created:

> In addition to interim due dates, I will spend more time in the beginning of the course teaching organizational and time-management skills. I will introduce course organizers as well as note-taking and short- and long-term organization techniques, and reinforce these concepts and skills throughout the course.

APPENDIX 3.1 — WEEK FOUR SURVEY: SURVEY FOR LOVRE'S CLASSES

This survey is to help explore both the strengths and weaknesses of the structure of this class. Please be thoughtful in answering the following questions. Your thoughtful honesty is the key to making this a meaningful way to improve this class.

1. Were the purposes of this system made clear to you?
    Very clear   Unclear
    5   4   3   2   1

    How?

2. Do you prioritize (or work on several) tasks in class?
    Always   Sometimes   Never
    5   4   3   2   1

    How does this affect your success?

3. How effectively do you use your *project time* in class?
    Very well   Not well
    5   4   3   2   1

4. How strong is the connection between your use of time in class and your learning?

    Very strong   Not strong
    5   4   3   2   1

5. Rate the usefulness of this system for your learning course content:

    Very useful   Not useful
    5   4   3   2   1

    Please explain:

6. Has this system taught you anything about the use of time and personal responsibility?

7. What are the strengths of this system?

8. How would you improve this system?

4

STUDENTS AS TEACHERS: A STUDY IN EFFECTIVENESS

Feather Alexander
Cedarcrest High School

Feather Alexander wanted to enlist her tenth grade English students as teachers of each other in her classroom. The 100-minute period gave her sufficient time, in her view, both "to 'cover' the curriculum and teach my students processes for having greater control over their own learning." Initially some students were enthusiastic about the new roles Alexander offered to them. Others resisted and felt that she was asking them to do her job. Alexander also experienced some resistance in herself to letting go of her control.

Could she learn how to structure "students as teachers" in such a way that the vast majority of students would both learn effectively and value this approach?

In her final effort in this term, she comments, "What began to emerge was a fully functioning, self-sustaining classroom in which students were actively participating and engaged in small groups." As students became more skilled as teachers, they increased their engagement in classroom activities not only in their teacher roles but also in their student roles.

100 MINUTES:
A CONTEXT FOR RESEARCH IN THE
ENGLISH CLASSROOM

Cedarcrest High School lies tucked away in the hills of Duvall, Washington, overlooking the Snoqualmie Valley, 30 miles east of Seattle. This tranquil setting is the backdrop for the high school where I teach English to students who come daily from the surrounding areas of Carnation and Duvall. Some come from their newly built homes in master-planned developments, and others from their farms, having fed the cows or chickens before boarding the bus. The school enrolls roughly 700 students.

Cedarcrest operates on a three-period day where students spend 100 minutes in each of three academic courses each term (45 days). Students also spend 37 minutes daily in an advisory program where they participate in schoolwide activities and club meetings and have time to study or access school resources such as the library or the computer lab. This schedule seems to work well by allowing students and teachers to focus on fewer subjects at the same time, thus encouraging students to concentrate more on the subjects that they are studying. In my two years teaching in this schedule, I have learned that a teacher must be creative and innovative when it comes to using instructional time. Given 100-minute lessons, this extended block of time should be used for extended thinking. Keeping this idea in mind, I chose a class that I would be teaching for the first time in which to develop a new way to structure the 100-minute block period.

The introduction to literature course is a tenth grade English requirement in which students are exposed to and re-

spond critically to different genres of literature. This course
helps students expand their analytical thinking and use rea-
soning to communicate in both written and oral formats.
These skills are critical for developing problem-solving and
critical thinking skills, which are necessary skills for students
preparing to enter a volatile workforce or a college experience. As an idealistic English teacher, it is also my hope that
exposure to the various meaningful and rich samples of literature will spark in my students a love of reading, which is so
critical in promoting life-long learning habits. To work toward these goals, I wanted to approach the curriculum in a
less conventional way, or at the least I wanted students to become more directly involved in the learning process. I initially hoped to create a classroom environment that catered
to what the students needed and wanted to learn, designed
partially by them, perhaps giving them a greater understanding of the course and of literature.

The goal of the course was to allow for greater student involvement in designing activities to help them learn about
poetry, short stories, novels, and plays. Not only did I want
students to be involved, I wanted them to participate in such
a way that the traditional notions of classroom roles would be
changed. The teacher's role would shift from being in control
of the learning to facilitating students who were in control of
their own learning. I planned to design activities where students became teachers of the content. In other words, students would actively define and assume the role of teacher in
this class. I initially thought that if students participated
more, they would learn and understand more about the critical concepts presented in the literature course.

The 100-minute block of time motivated me to try giving
students more control of classroom activities. Before beginning the study, I knew that this approach would require more
time than if I were to remain in control of all activities. However, because I had 100 minutes to work with each day, I felt
that there was sufficient time to cover the curriculum and
teach my students processes for having greater control over
their own learning. The extended block of time not only gave
me an opportunity for innovation that a short period would
not, but it necessitated this innovation. To maintain student

attention and interest for 100 minutes, variety and creativity are vital. What better way to get them interested than to have them become directly involved in how the material is taught?

To find out what would help to maximize learning and to use time in an innovative manner, I pursued these research questions:

- ♦ How can the use of "students as teachers" be effective in the 100-minute period?
- ♦ How does this shift from traditional roles enhance students' learning and understanding?

To answer these questions, I used action-research methodology. I designed a study set in the context of my own classroom. By looking reflectively at my teaching methods, I hoped to find ways to improve my use of the block period. The practice of observing my own teaching and revising it to facilitate student learning was key. The excitement of the study was that it was designed to work within the context of my classroom, and it was developed to promote my growth and improvement as a teacher. The study was undertaken to see if my idea for restructuring roles and time in a block period class would work. And the result would be to tell the story of what went on within my classroom with the hopes that it would inform my practice and prove useful to other teachers in block schedules.

My plan was to begin by asking myself what the traditional classroom roles were and how they were defined by me and by my students. Then, in collaboration with the students, I would devise ways of changing those roles. Various activities would be developed throughout the course to encourage more student involvement. As a class, we would be able to identify the reasons for more student involvement, link student participation to specific elements of the curriculum, create criteria for student involvement, and reflect on and assess our progress at various points along the way. The action research approach would allow us to journey through the term, employing the classroom as a learning lab of sorts, as we voyaged to discover effective methods of using time for learning, enacting our new roles.

To gather the data that tells the story of what went on within my classroom walls, I collected student and teacher journal responses, notes from classroom discussions, and an initial and final survey completed by my students. These sources of data were invaluable in gathering the perceptions and understandings of those involved in the activities. The data helped to point to what was thought to be effective and useful in terms of learning by the students and by the teacher. And as we paused and reflected on our progress at various points during the term, the data helped to inform the research design itself. Homework, essays, and projects created as a result of the activities also helped to illumine what the students had learned and could express. Ultimately, the data reveal student and teacher attitudes about the course activities and about teaching and learning. It is these very attitudes which help to answer the question of effectiveness posed by my research.

A Study in Teaching and Learning

Students entering my classroom on the first day of the term were greeted with sheets of butcher paper lining the walls. At the top of each sheet of paper, a single word was written, each word one of the critical concepts for the course. These pages included terms such as *poetry, novel, reading*, and *writing,* but some key concepts for the study were also included, such as *teaching* and *learning.* Students were each given a colored marker and were asked to walk around the room, without talking to their classmates, and write words or phrases which they associated with each of the terms listed on the butcher paper. The point of the lesson was not to come to formal definitions on the first day but to get students immediately involved and to share their thoughts about these key concepts. After students had responded in writing, we discussed each term to provide a context for the course and for the study. Students had a sense for what they would learn, and they also were able to express initial impressions of traditional classroom roles. Their first impressions indicated that they viewed the teacher as primarily the *keeper of knowledge* and the student as the *receiver of information.* I had expected students to respond this way, which provided a good starting point from which we could define the shift of roles in this course.

Students were told on the first day that they would be responsible for teaching portions of the course. So as not to put any individual on the spot and to emphasize cooperative skills, I decided that students would be responsible for teaching and presenting information in small groups of four to six students. To encourage students to teach the course content effectively, I first had to ask the students how they defined good teaching. Students individually, and then collectively, came up with a list of defining traits and characteristics of a good teacher. We discussed the issue as a class and then determined that to keep groups accountable for good teaching, they would be graded based upon the quality of their presentation and the effectiveness of their lesson.

Students were then given the task of developing a rubric for teaching. The class was split into five groups, and each was assigned a letter grade: A, B, C, D, or F. The task of each group was to develop criteria for assessing teaching at that letter-grade level, which would then be applied to their presentations for the remainder of the term. The students took this task quite seriously and really grappled with questions of distinctions, such as what makes a B different from an A or a C. Each group presented its criteria and also acted out a scenario in which a teacher would deserve such a grade. This was helpful for illustrative purposes to guide students' preparation for their own teaching experiences. The criteria for each grade were then discussed with the whole class, and revisions were made together which we could all accept.

This student-created rubric (see Appendix 4.1, p. 106) was then used to evaluate presentations for the remainder of the term. Each student had a copy, and because students were actively involved in the development of the criteria, the guidelines were known and clear to all. This activity was important in that it defined the expectations for students' own teaching experiences. Most importantly, the teacher did not set the criteria for them; the students themselves created the guidelines for teaching that they would seek to enact. My role to this point was to question and guide their development of ideas.

Poetry: The First Assignment

After receiving an introduction to the genre of poetry from me, reading and responding to some poetic samples as a class, and learning literary terms of importance, students were ready for their first teaching experience. Until this point, I had assumed the traditional role of teacher in charge of the activities and the learning. I found myself somewhat reluctant to give up the control of the class even though I expected that having students teach the class would be worthwhile. My reluctance seemed to stem from my own ambivalence and concern. This was a completely new approach, and I guess I was still questioning how effective it would be. How would the students understand if I didn't tell them what onomatopoeia means? Or how would they dissect and interpret a poem if I didn't ask the right questions? I wanted them to be able to define, explain, and question each other. I thought that if they taught the class, all students would become more engaged with the material, but I feared that they would not help each other learn enough or in enough depth. Yet I knew I had to push these fears aside and dive into the experience.

For their first teaching experience, students were reminded of the rubric for teaching that they had created. I then assigned them to groups, so that students would not work with their friends for this activity. I also wanted each group to have a range of ability levels and talents. Each group was given a different poem, with instructions to read it, to come to an understanding of the poem as a group, and then to devise a way to teach it to the rest of the class. Before students prepared their lessons, we discussed together some concerns and ideas to keep in mind. Students reiterated the criteria for quality teaching that they deemed important. They noted that their presentations of the poems needed to be informative yet fun, and had to include a component that got the rest of the class involved in learning about and responding to the poem.

Each group was given time to prepare its lesson plan. As the groups prepared, I made myself available for assistance in interpreting the poems and for coaching in planning teaching activities. My goal was to give the student groups ownership of the material and the teaching while offering advice for making sure that all group members had a role in understanding the material and preparing to teach it. While the students were in this initial planning phase, I was unsure of how their lessons would work, but I had faith that this would be a worthwhile experience. And it seemed that students were working together and keeping each other attentive to the task at-hand. The cooperative approach seemed well suited to the activity because it was a meaningful activity in which each person had to be involved, as each would be held accountable for an understanding of a poem when she or he stood in front of the class as a teacher.

After the students had prepared their lessons, they were ready to present. The class was reminded of the teaching rubric, and the students were told to give each group a grade after experiencing their presentation of the material. The students approached this first teaching experience with almost the same youthful enthusiasm that I have in approaching my own teaching. I was a bit anxious to see how this would go, but I did not lead the procession of activities. I simply designated the order in which the groups would teach their poems and then I sat back, ready to learn. As I listened to the groups present their information and explain and lead various fairly creative activities to involve the rest of the class, I was impressed with their preparation. I especially enjoyed the variety of activities among the groups. Each group made sure that its approach was different from the others. One group had created quiz show-type games in which the class' knowledge of the poem was tested. Another had the class create a group poem that mirrored the style of its poem. The next group had individuals respond to a theme in the poem by writing similes, while another individual led a discussion of personal connections to the poem. All the activities seemed to engage most of the class.

The students had clearly decided to meet the challenge of teaching their poems well. Of course, this being their first time, there were areas that could be improved. Many of the groups focused on telling the rest of the class what they thought their poem meant rather than asking questions that would challenge their peers to come to their own conclusions. Some groups lacked focus, while several members of the class did not pay attention or participate the entire time.

While the groups continued to present, I attempted to divorce myself from my urge to take over the class, clarify the poems, and give new direction to the assignments and activities. Even though this first attempt at teaching was a bit rocky, it seemed to be a worthwhile experience. Each group clearly knew the poem they were presenting, and most of the students were actively involved in each lesson, although the degree of involvement varied greatly from student to student.

Although I perceived this activity to be generally effective, with some obvious needs for improvement, I wanted to know what the students thought. Did they enjoy the activity? Did they think it helped them learn about these poems? I asked them two simple questions following the activity:

- ♦ What went well?
- ♦ What do we need to work on?

These questions generated some candid and thoughtful written responses from the students, which they also shared aloud in a whole-class discussion. Many common themes emerged from this first set of responses. When asked what went well, most students agreed on these points:

- ♦ Participation was a key part of teaching the class.
- ♦ Everyone had participated in their group's presentation.
- ♦ They had put much effort into ensuring that their presentation was informative and understandable to others.
- ♦ They had to cooperate effectively in order to be well-prepared.

They also hinted at the fact that they had to think critically about the poem they were presenting in order to present good ideas that were informed and that involved such higher-order thinking skills as understanding, interpretation, analysis, and explanation. Students also noted that the groups' strategies for presenting information were effective in that there was variety among groups. All groups did a good job of "reading their poems...loud and clear" for the class, yet the way they got the whole class involved varied from a game to a group discussion to assigning the students to write their own collective poem. A few students even went so far as to say that the activity was fun. One student explained that the activity went well because when students teach each other, "we don't just sit there and hear a lecture." Thus, the active involvement was engaging for the students.

When asked what we needed to work on, the students had many good suggestions. Overwhelmingly, they noted that the class needed to be quiet and work on listening to a group that was attempting to teach. Others noted that the class needed to participate actively, without complaints, when they were the students as well as the teachers. Many students claimed that this was an issue of respect. The class as a whole needed to show more respect for every teaching group. They also noted that there were tasks that they could do better in terms of their teaching. They explained that being better organized and clearer when presenting information would help them to better understand each other. Planning for variety and in-depth understanding were also noted as important. They did not want their lessons to be boring or confusing. Students noted that to make these improvements they would need more practice as teachers: more time to prepare and present their lessons so that they were not rushed. They would also need a way to make sure that all group members were equally involved in the preparation of the lesson. One student mentioned her frustration with feeling that she had done all of the work. She noted that smaller working groups would help to distribute tasks more equitably. Students also seemed to think that more accountability would help reduce disruption in the class. One student offered this suggestion: "Perhaps next time when written involvement from the class is asked for, they could also be handed in and graded. Many people felt no need to write when asked." Many groups had prepared wonderful activities for involving the class but did not get full participation because the students lacked accountability.

Finally, students discussed improving their attitudes about sharing ideas. While one student explained that it was interesting to hear different views on subjects, many students noted that various individuals became frustrated with each other when they had differing opinions. People were "talking out of turn" and "arguing about stupid things," noted one student. Several students noted that the solution to this problem would be for everyone to have patience.

After only one teaching experience, it was interesting to note that students were able to identify strengths and weaknesses and could reflect on their activities and point to ways of improving. It seemed intriguing that the aspects they pointed to affect me as a teacher when I present a lesson as well. This affirmed to me that their teaching experiences were genuine.

SECOND IMPRESSIONS

After the poetry unit, I was excited to give students more opportunities to teach each other. But for some reason, I pushed on through the short story unit and the drama unit, and I had plowed through the first play without giving the students much further opportunity for teaching. Students had been given many opportunities for sharing their ideas with each other, but this was informal and did not quite meet the scope of the research. Although this project had been by my design, I found it difficult to give up control of the class because that meant giving up time and possibly content. I felt pressured to teach the many concepts of the course instead of letting the students experience them and teach each other.

By the time we were halfway through the drama unit, students had only read parts of the stories and the play aloud and had discussed the material by sharing projects they had created. These activities were their only means of active participation since the poetry teaching groups. Although I had fallen away from the project somewhat, at this point I administered an initial survey in which I asked students to respond to their teaching experience to this point in the course and to give me feedback that would guide the next teaching activity. With this initial survey, I was attempting to gather their responses to being involved in teaching parts of the course. I also planned to survey them again at the close of the study to see if their attitudes and opinions had changed.

Students were asked to respond to the following statements by agreeing or disagreeing to varying degrees (see Appendix 4.2, p. 107, for the complete survey):

♦ Teaching portions of this class is worthwhile.

Of the 26 students who completed the survey, 16 (62%) agreed with this statement. Students explained that it could be beneficial as long as respect and group participation are the goals. Students also noted that they had to know a lot about the subject in order to teach it, and once they had experienced the frustration of some students not listening, they empathized with how the adult teacher feels. Many thought it was worthwhile because they were able to see points of view other than the teacher's. As one student commented, "Teaching ourselves allows us to teach in ways other than how the teacher teaches. Everyone has different learning styles and this way more learning styles can be met." Others simply noted that they liked the change of pace. Some listed practical reasons why it was worthwhile: "It helps us get ready for presentations or job interviews in the future," one wrote.

Although the majority of students agreed that teaching the class was worthwhile, some felt that the student presentations were not as "high quality" or as structured as what they received from a teacher. One student simply said he did not like working with others and did not respect his peers as much as adults. Others noted that as high school students they did not feel prepared to teach each other because they had not yet "gone to college."

♦ I like being involved in teaching portions of this class.

Nineteen students (73%) agreed with this statement. Many indicated similar reasons as they had noted in response to the first statement. This implied that when an activity was seen as worthwhile, it was also deemed enjoyable. Students commented that they enjoyed teaching portions of the class because it got everyone involved, allowed them to share ideas, helped them to learn, added "a bit of a twist," and was fun and interesting. Those who did not particularly like teaching said that they did not like getting up in front of the class, or that they did not learn as much because the lessons were not as well structured as they were with traditional classroom roles.

♦ Working together in groups helps me to learn.

Twenty students (77%) agreed with this statement. This statement got the greatest amount of agreement from the class. This response indicated to me that student team-teaching in small groups was a good configuration. Most of the students indicated that this was a helpful way to learn because they could share and discuss various ideas and interpretations. One student's comment explained why hearing what others had to say was important: "Because there is more than just one opinion of an answer." Several students said that getting input or feedback from others was crucial. Students also said that they learned communication and social skills such as listening and respecting ideas. The only comments that indicated a need for improvement focused on the need to have groups that were small enough to allow for meaningful discussion. The students indicated that a group size of two to four people was ideal.

♦ Working together is a good way to teach the class.

Seventeen students (65%) agreed with this statement. Again, the majority of the students agreed with this but not as strongly as they had agreed with the value of working together as a learning activity (see the previous question). Students enjoyed the fact that they were not "put on the spot" by being asked to teach alone. They also indicated that this type of activity caused some students to share who "might not have spoken up on their own." Students liked the variety created by this type of activity and felt they could understand lessons prepared by student groups because "we think on the same level as most of our classmates." A few students, however, indicated that some students confuse the class and a lesson could be taught more thoroughly and concisely by a "real teacher."

For the most part, the students' initial responses were quite positive. They also responded on the survey by listing activities that they thought to be helpful for learning, and they defined when learning was fun. Students indicated that they needed to participate in hands-on or group activities in order to learn. Many students also favored large group discussions. All of these activities were said to be helpful because they involved doing things that were creative, active, and interesting. Students wanted to be able to connect topics of study in the classroom to their own lives. Students said that learning was fun when everyone participated, when they understood, when they could get up and move around, when it went at a fast pace, and when it "felt good." These categorizations of helpful and fun informed the rest of the study by guiding me to devise lessons which embodied the qualities and elements that students had associated with each of them.

JULIUS CAESAR: TEACHING THROUGH ACTING

After the students had given me such informed and honest feedback, I was compelled to provide them with another opportunity to teach the class. Our next play, *Julius Caesar*, proved to be a good opportunity to do so. As we began this play, students grumbled and groaned about not wanting to read it. Protests such as "I can't understand it," "This is in English?" and "Why are you making me read this?" echoed through my classroom. The last one really got me. The students felt they had lost their sense of ownership in the course, and the participatory nature of the classroom seemed to be fading fast. I knew I had to do something to make them feel more involved and connected to the play, while at the same time, reviewing the story line for those who had become confused by the language.

Because the play has five acts, the students were assigned to five different groups. Each group was responsible for creating and presenting a newscast that outlined the major events of the act. The presentation had to be organized, informative, and creative. All group members had to participate. The class discussed the components of a newscast—top story, features, weather report, anchors, field reporters, and so on—and decided they would have to present a variety of stories in order to capture the events of each act fully. This activity would allow students to teach each other in a new and creative way, one much more interesting than a teacher-directed worksheet or review session.

Each group was given time to meet, prepare, and present its broadcast. The results were phenomenal. Each group participated and was prepared to an extent that indicated its members fully understood the events of the play. The presentations were spread throughout our study of the play; each group presented after we had finished reading its act. This pacing helped alleviate the rushed and repetitive feeling of scheduling all of the group presentations on the same day, which we had done in the poetry unit.

Students also debriefed this activity by assessing the work of their own group. They commented in writing about how well they thought they had done. They believed that their knowledge of their act and incorporation of all of its scenes into their presentation were strong. They felt good about the clear, creative quality of their presentations in which all group members had participated. Students noted that they had prepared a variety of news stories and had thought them through, many preparing written scripts. They also pointed out that they had used good public-speaking skills such as eye contact, loud voices, and visual aids. Students said that they saw improvements in their ability to teach each other in terms of organization and confidence in front of the group.

The biggest weakness identified by students was that individual group members were not always equal participants. However, students noted that their ability to work together and present information were improving: "Best of all, our group didn't argue and we had a good time."

Once the students began to identify and reflect upon their ability to work together to create and offer a presentation, they began to see their own growth and to find that this work was an enjoyable experience that had merit in terms of their learning.

NIGHT: LITERATURE GROUPS

The student-led teaching activities that I had facilitated thus far in the course had been effective, but I felt that I still had not relinquished enough control of the class. These teaching activities had allowed for students to figure out what works in terms of conveying information, but this was still more limited than I wanted their experience to be. For the final novel of the course, *Night*, I devised an activity that would allow students to teach each other in a two-faceted approach: the literature group.

A literature group consists of five students, each of whom has a unique role or job each day. The students had to read from 10 to 20 pages each night, complete a designated task, and bring their work to class ready to share with their group. Each individual's job was different, so the group was counting on each individual to be prepared in order to understand its reading fully. The jobs for the literature groups were:

- Question writer: writes at least five questions for discussion
- Vocabulary finder: finds, defines, and uses in a sentence five new words from the reading.
- Story mapper: maps out (recounts) the elements of the plot. This could be a paragraph or a web or some other graphic representation.
- Illustrator: illustrates a key scene and explains its importance.
- Performer: chooses a key passage, reads it aloud to the group, and explains its significance.

Each job had a written component to be completed and placed in a group portfolio, and each individual was required to meet and share his or her work with the group daily. This structure made students accountable because they had a product to turn in, and it gave them items for discussion. Because each individual had a different job, all students were teaching their small group about some aspect of the reading about which they had become an expert. This provided a chance for individual teaching, but it was informal and done in a small group so students seemed more comfortable. Students devised a plan within their group to rotate jobs so that they would each get a chance to experience doing each job. They were accountable daily for completing their jobs because I came around to each group and checked for completion. Students were also accountable to their group for doing thoughtful work, because they were compiling their job assignments to create a group portfolio.

The literature groups were a good teaching activity because the jobs were interesting to students and often required in-depth and divergent thinking. It was at this point that students started to assume more control of their own learning. They began monitoring each other's behavior in the literature groups, focusing to keep everyone on task. They also began to check and offer revisions on the individual jobs that each group member had done. This was prompted by the fact that the group members would each receive the same grade for the collaborative portfolio.

What began to emerge was a fully functioning, self-sustaining classroom in which students actively participated and engaged in small groups. Real teaching and learning were occurring, and I was on the side, both coaching and watching it all happen.

The second facet of teaching involved with the literature groups was that each group was not only responsible for completing all jobs, meeting daily to share information, and compiling a portfolio; they were also responsible for creating and administering a quiz and leading a whole-group discussion for one specific section of the reading. This aspect of the literature groups completed the role reversal for which I had hoped. Indeed, more than a simple role reversal, all participants in the classroom were experiencing an expansion of their previous roles. The students had become teachers as well as learners, and I had become a coach and a learner as well as a direct instructor of content and skills. My job at this point was to monitor the groups, make sure individuals were accountable, answer questions, and provide structure (a reading schedule, group assignments, schedule of presentations and quizzes). Many of my duties were administrative. The students were in charge of their own learning, both in the small groups and in the large group. Students worked together and created quizzes for the reading which were challenging and thoughtful. Many times the questions were more difficult than questions I would have asked. After giving the quiz, each group was responsible for grading the assignment and reporting the results to me. Thus, they retained control of the concepts to be learned and assessed.

The whole-group discussions led by the small groups were also fairly informative. The students asked factual questions as well as opinion questions. Because the subject matter of the novel evoked many emotions, students also discussed the themes of religion, racism, and persecution. Students often asked their peers to imagine what they would have done if they had been among the prisoners of the concentration camps. Several emotional and challenging discussions resulted from the thoughtfully prepared questions.

I struggled with the question of what my role in this class should be. I wanted the students to have control, but I also wanted them to learn that such blatant examples of hate are not a joking matter. During the discussions, some students were making light of the questions being posed and offering flippant remarks. Others were still not participating in the discussions or were being disruptive. I tried to stay detached and see how the student/teachers would handle this. They did fairly well with trying to keep each other on task because they had been practicing this in the small groups. But the large-group dynamics became at times unmanageable. Although all individuals would have their turn in front of the group as teacher, when individuals were acting as students rather than as teachers they sometimes forgot what it was like to be in front of the group. Although I claimed to have handed over control fully at this point, I did step in a few times to offer my opinions on the topics of conversation in an attempt to steer the talk toward tolerance and understanding.

While there were a few uncomfortable moments in the whole-group discussions, I gauged the activity to be a great learning experience. Some of the intolerant remarks and attitudes almost had to be brought up in order for students to grapple with the weight of the emotions surrounding a Holocaust account. It seemed also that students learned more about tolerance for others in a conceptual sense, as they struggled with learning how to be respectful toward their peers who were leading any given activity.

Throughout the term with the gradual building of student responsibility and control of the learning process, it was interesting to see that students also gradually assumed more control of the management of behavior. Though disruptions remained a major concern throughout the course, they began to diminish, and the way they were dealt with began to change. In the beginning of the course, when I was reluctant to give up my control of the class, I would assume the traditional role of teacher and step in to discipline the group when disruptions of the lesson became a problem. However, by the end of the term, students had begun to monitor each other. For example, during the last unit, a student wrote an unsolicited letter to the class expressing her concerns over behavior during the class discussions. She asked me to read the following letter aloud to the class:

> Dear Class,
>
> I am very disappointed in how we are acting. We are all being very rude to the groups who are trying to present. I wish everyone would stop talking and be respectful. I don't want to get in front of you and be rudely ignored. It makes people very frustrated to not have people listen to you. Could we please be quiet and listen so we can learn and get things done?
>
> Thanks,
>
> A concerned student

The letter demonstrated that this student, who voiced the concerns of a good number of her peers, thought that the activities in which we were engaged and the ideas we were exploring were important; enough so to speak up and tell her classmates that she wanted to learn without interruption. Her letter also indicated that full participation by the members of the class was important to the outcome of the activities. Unfortunately, the classroom roles had not been completely transformed, because it was still my job as the teacher to relay this information and the student did not feel comfortable enough to give her identity to the group. However, the class seemed to consider her request rather than shun it, as they might have done had I simply expressed my own concerns.

FINAL THOUGHTS: THE STUDENTS REFLECT

After they had participated in the various activities ranging from little to large amounts of responsibility for their own learning, the students completed a final activity in which they reflected on their experience with teaching various portions of the course. Students completed an exit survey identical to the survey completed earlier (see Appendix 4.2, p. 107). They also compiled a list of definitions of key terms and participated in a culminating whole-class discussion over these two items. I wanted them to tell me what they had gained from participating in teaching parts of the class.

When asked to complete a second survey, student responses differed slightly from the initial survey. Though I perceived the class to have learned more from enacting more responsibility throughout the course, the students seemed to be less enthusiastic in their second response to the survey questions. Though the percentages had decreased, the students still overwhelmingly agreed with each of the following statements, indicating that, for the most part, they found that teaching the class was a rewarding experience.

♦ Teaching portions of this class is worthwhile.

Of the 26 students who responded, 17 (65%) agreed with this statement. Students said that they were able to learn from each other and found it worthwhile that they were given a chance to teach. Some students noted that the traditional teacher should not be the only one teaching, and that students should not be the only ones learning, indicating that the role expansion I had hoped for had taken place. Others thought it was a fun and effective means for helping them to see things at their own level of understanding. One student even noted that she "learned a lot and liked having the responsibility." Finally, students noted that it helped them to interact with each other and to develop good team working habits.

Some students were frustrated with the process at this point and noted that it "needs work" and that at times it seemed chaotic and frustrating when not everyone paid attention. This made some students view the activity as "stressful and a waste of time." While many indicated that the experience was difficult, most said they had learned from it.

♦ I like being involved in teaching portions of this class.

Sixteen of the 26 students (62%) agreed with this statement. Students said that they enjoyed the teaching activities because they learned more and became confident in front of a group. Students enjoyed the collaborative and hands-on aspects of becoming more involved in teaching the class and noted that this engaged the entire class in participating in the course content. They said it could be fun; therefore they liked doing it. Many linked the worthwhile nature of the activity to whether or not they liked doing it. One student said "everyone should get a chance to learn how to teach," while another said he liked it because "we understand [the course content] better from our own age group."

Those who did not like teaching parts of the course said it was a waste of time because they were not always given the respect they felt they needed from their peers. Others said it would have been better had the entire class become fully involved. One student had difficulty accepting the shift from traditional roles: "I prefer to learn rather than teach when I enter a class. Traditionally, I came to be taught." Another student simply said it was "boring," and that he saw no relevance to future activities. Most students liked being involved and offered suggestions for improvement.

♦ Working together in groups helps me to learn.

Eighteen of the 26 students (69%) agreed with this statement. Students said it helped that they were able to talk about the material in groups and hear others' ideas and input. Some said that this was the best way to learn. Others said that they learned better by themselves because they were easily distracted in groups, or they felt that they had to do others' share of the work when a group task was assigned. This was still the statement that generated the most agreement from the students.

♦ Working together is a good way for us to teach the class.

Sixteen of the 26 students (62%) agreed with this statement. Students said that they were able to hear different ideas and learn from each other by putting "a bunch of ideas together to form one concept." Students said that the teaching involved students and helped them to learn more, perhaps because they were able to understand each other better. One student clearly summarized why it was effective: "Because all of us can teach better than one."

Those who did not think it was effective said that it was difficult to teach in large groups because not everyone really participated. They also said that it was not effective when other students did not pay attention, participate, or do their share of the work.

When asked what helped them to learn, students cited many of the same activities they had referred to on the initial survey. They said that hands-on activities, group discussions, and working together were helpful as long as "there is understanding." Others noted that they needed visual parts of a lesson, or that they needed to see a connection—"material I can use in life." However, an overwhelming number of students stated that activities that were fun and got the class involved helped them the most.

When asked what made learning fun, students said that participation, effort, and involvement by the whole class made learning enjoyable. Others said that a challenging lesson was fun. While none of the students came right out and said that learning is fun when they are teaching, many alluded to times when teaching the class had been a fun experience. Students said that learning is fun when everyone gets along, when "I enjoy the subject I'm working on with friends," "when we learn something from the teaching," "when we get to be involved," and "when students get involved in helping everyone out." These comments indicated that students seemed to enjoy not only the collaborative aspect of the course, but that they also enjoyed getting involved in the course by teaching parts of it. Finally, they seemed to enjoy the fact that the teaching activities had a positive effect upon overall participation in the classroom.

As part of organizing final thoughts on the study, I asked students to define six key terms in their own words: teacher, student, effectiveness, learning, understanding, and teaching. I instructed them to create definitions based on their experiences in the course, and I asked them to list any other key words that helped to define their experience with teaching. By asking the students to tell me in their own words the meaning of these key terms, I hoped to see how effectively I had shifted from traditional roles, how much ownership they felt, and, ultimately, how effective the teaching activities had been. The following is a compilation of student definitions. Some responses, which were quite similar, have been merged.

- ♦ Teacher: someone who teaches or instructs; an adult figure who can teach the class as a whole; one who assigns activities; one who puts forth much effort to accurately portray new material; a person who, no matter what difficulties come along, gives it their all; a person who leads and makes a class learn; a person or group who is teaching the class about something they have researched; telling about a topic by means of showing, playing, or discussing; a person who explains something to someone; someone you can talk to and trust, someone who will listen and advise; someone who tries their best to help students learn through various means; helps students get organized and helps students in the learning process; the teacher and the students who participated in the teaching activities throughout the term.

- ♦ Student: someone who learns; person who is taught; applies learned knowledge given by the teacher; a person who is doing work for an instructor; a person who gets and remembers information; someone who should strive to do their best and to understand that they have to try; a student should listen to the teacher and respect the teacher; the one who is following directions; listens, participates, and shares ideas; comes to school to learn skills necessary to survive competitively in the world outside the classroom; anyone who is learning something from someone else; person being taught by a teacher or in some occasions by themselves; lazy and whiny; studies and investigates; interacts in learning activities; has an open mind.

♦ Effectiveness: how well a student or teacher learns; the way you do things versus the way others do things; producing the desired effect, or the making of an impression on one's mind; reviewing and discussing; being able to carry out a task thoroughly and completely with a positive approach; how well something impacts something; it works really well and serves its purpose; when the class learns everything that needed to be taught; when you teach someone something and they can tell it in their own words; retaining knowledge, inventive; putting in ideas; when something works to everyone's advantage; the ability to get through to the students; understanding, completion; efficient; degree of preciseness with which something gets done; when something is put to good use and not wasted.

♦ Learning: to help expand one's mind; what the student does in class and at home, as well as the teacher; to acquire knowledge or skill; understanding something new; comprehending; remembering information; bringing in information that you didn't know before; absorbing information, thoughts, and feelings; processing information through acting, reading, and writing; meant to improve ourselves as individuals and as a whole; being told something and being able to know it afterwards; portraying new concepts to people who can then teach someone else about it, which means they understand; the process of expanding your knowledge; accepting new material and giving it your best to comprehend and apply; ability to write one's own interpretation; when one or more pieces of information sticks in your brain.

♦ Understanding: when a student/teacher knows what they are talking about; being able to know the material; if you are learning, you are understanding; the power to think and learn, intelligence; does not happen when students become bored; taking what you have learned and grasping its meaning and function; listening and comprehending; when someone teaches you about something and you can effectively use it in your life; knowing what the thing you learned means; being able to use acquired information; acceptance, lenience; knowing what must be done and accomplishing it to your full potential; being able to figure out what is being taught; being able to take into account what is being learned; getting it; when one has grasped a concept.

♦ Teaching: to help a student learn and understand; an action done by students and teacher alike; sharing knowledge; showing the class what they need to know; talking about what you have learned with others; helping others learn new things that they can apply; relaying information; showing and receiving respect; explaining something new; getting the lesson across to the students; does not involve just the teacher—we are open to ideas and we learn from others teaching and what we teach ourselves; the process of informing a

person or group of people on a subject or idea
which you are knowledgeable on; taking what
you have learned and then helping someone else
to grasp the same understanding; providing insight; helping to expand the students' minds;
when the class is cooperative and learns and understands something new.

Given these student definitions, I believe I can reasonably
assert the following conclusions about our experience in this
study. Many of the key concepts defined by these students in
relation to teaching and learning have become enmeshed in
each other; they are more integral and connected and less
separate and distinct. This quality in students' definitions
suggests that the traditional teacher/student roles in this
classroom were transformed in some significant way; that
teaching and learning were conducted by all participants in
the classroom; and that respect, participation, and cooperation were important aspects of this transformation. I believe
that the students learned not only the critical course concepts
but also a significant amount about teaching and learning.

SUMMARY OF FINDINGS AND
IMPLICATIONS FOR FURTHER RESEARCH

Conducting a study in one's own classroom is an enlightening experience. As a teacher it caused me to reflect continu-
ally upon my practice in order to improve. It also made my
students constantly aware that we were doing and trying
new things, and this outlook, while it caused all of us to
struggle through some unknowns, proved to be effective in
developing critical thinking capacities in all of us as we challenged ourselves to grow and learn.

In conducting this study, I was asking how the use of students as teachers can be effective in the 100-minute block period and how this shift from traditional roles can help to enhance students' learning and understanding. The first issue
that this question looks at is time. Because a class period lasts
for 100 minutes, I knew alternative approaches had to be
used to engage the students. As they put it, sitting for 100

minutes gets boring. The teaching activities, because they required collaboration and usually involved moving about, discussing, and creating products were definitely good uses of the longer period. The extended period of time facilitated turning the class over to students because it allowed for group meetings and preparation, student-presented lessons, and debriefing time usually within one class period. The extended block of time also allowed for more in-depth discussions and for meaningful chunks of time that could be devoted to small group meetings. In addition, it allowed me to coach and monitor all groups on the same day. Because of the 100-minute block, I was able to monitor and gauge where all students were each day. The variety and growth that teaching each other provided for the students seemed to be a beneficial use of time for them as well.

The study worked on the premise that much of the control of the class would be shifted from me to the students. At first, I had a difficult time doing this. I had trouble stepping out of my traditionally defined role of being in charge of every aspect of the course. However, as time went on and students became more successful at teaching each other, I believe that we achieved an expansion of our roles that was marked by a new balance. Within this balance I gave up much or even most of the control of the classroom, and my students accepted significantly higher levels of responsibility for their own learning. Interestingly, at the same time that I was hesitant to relinquish control of my classroom, my students seemed unable to expand their traditional roles within the classroom. But by the end of the term, I had let go significantly, and they had grown dramatically. Within this new balance, I provided students with a context and a framework for teaching and learning, and I insisted on both group and individual accountability. I also monitored students' efforts and accomplishments. My students had become effective teachers of their peers as well as more successful learners.

Did allowing the students to teach portions of the class help them to learn better and understand more of the course content? Yes, I believe so. Students noted that the types of activities and the collaborative nature of the course helped them to understand the content in greater depth, though at times it was difficult to learn because of disorganization. In looking at the effectiveness of using students as teachers in the classroom, we must look at three key concepts: collaboration, participation, and respect.

Students for the most part indicated that collaboration was an extremely helpful part of their teaching experience. Students not only felt more comfortable presenting lessons as a group, but they enjoyed the chance to see their peers' perspectives as they approached different concepts. Many students felt they learned more from each other because material was presented at their level of understanding. Students not only learned more about the curriculum by working together, but they also learned invaluable lessons about teamwork and about how much effort is required by each individual in order for a team to be successful.

Intermingled with collaboration was the issue of participation, which students strongly valued. They clearly indicated that for a group to be successful, each member of the group had to participate fully. However, students also indicated that when a small group of students was teaching, real learning was not occurring unless the entire class participated in the lesson and tried to learn. Students felt frustrated and less effective when class participation was not 100%. This notion of total participation in order to achieve optimum learning seemed to indicate how high the sense of ownership was in the classroom. Most students wanted everyone to succeed, and participation was crucial for understanding, learning, and success.

Finally, the issue of respect was important throughout the course. Students indicated time and again that a lack of participation in a student-led activity indicated a lack of respect. Overall, there were some minor problems with the class not fully respecting a group that was attempting to teach. Also at first, student groups that were teaching became frustrated and lost patience with their classmates. Though the students improved in this area, the issue of respect was never fully resolved. Students wanted respect from each other but did not always give it. I did not always step in, because I wanted students to figure it out on their own. If nothing else, the fact that respect was such a big issue taught the students to empathize with their teachers, because they had experienced first hand the difficulty in attempting to present a lesson when students were not respectful.

As we worked out how students would teach each other, we came up with two very important distinctions that helped us define teaching roles. When a group presented a lesson to the class, we stressed the importance of active involvement and tried to determine the difference between "telling" and "teaching." Students' first instincts were to "tell" others all about something that they had prepared and about which they were well informed. But we decided as a result of these initial teaching efforts that "just saying it" does not mean you are teaching. Students were able to verbalize at the end of the course that teaching means involving students, getting to the point quickly, asking and answering questions, and working toward understanding. Teaching, they determined, was effective, whereas telling was not.

Also, as students taught each other, especially in the literature groups, we tried to distinguish between "showing" others what you know or have completed and "sharing" this information with a group. When students first began meeting in literature groups to discuss the reading and to teach each other about the jobs they had completed, their first instinct was to show the others quickly what they had done and move on, so as to proceed through the activity without really giving much thought to what they were doing. We discussed why we were meeting in literature groups, and why it was important to share rather than show information. We decided that showing meant simply telling others to look for themselves at what you had done. On the other hand, we said that sharing was more effective because it involved giving thoughts, responses, and input about something they had created. Sharing seemed to facilitate discussion and create a larger understanding of the subject. Unlike merely showing others a piece of writing or a drawing, sharing meant explaining, discussing, and learning. Simply getting through an activity did not ensure that everyone understood; we needed to discuss and share in order to learn.

Letting students teach the class proved overall to be a great experience for everyone involved and a good way to use the longer block of time. In the future, when I ask students to become teachers, there are a few methods I will change, based upon this study. First, I will give up more control earlier in the course by providing students with activities and options for teaching each other. The literature group approach, where students teach each other in a small group and then also team-teach the whole class, is a good way to do this. Giving up more control will help the students to have more responsibility for the course content, yet maintaining variety will be crucial so that students will not be bored with teaching. A good balance of activities and responsibilities is important, so that the students have fun and learn from the activities.

Secondly, although we discussed criteria for good teaching, did role-playing exercises, and discussed how we would approach the teaching aspect of the class, we did not do as good a job clarifying student responsibilities. This created some initial tension and some problems with respect throughout the course. When I ask students to be teachers in the future, we will also clarify the criteria for good listening and appropriate behavior when a group of students is teaching. I hope to devise a way to make students accountable not only for listening to their peers but also for participating fully, perhaps by also giving them a grade in this area, or, better yet, by asking them to assess themselves based on criteria that they themselves have established.

Lastly, I plan to use the results of this study to encourage myself to let students become more actively involved. By allowing them to teach the course, I feel they learned so much more about literature, communication, learning, each other, and themselves. Giving students the responsibility of teaching challenges them to know and understand the material being studied. Looking at new ways to use an extended period has caused me to want to continue to practice reflective teaching and to continue to use the method of students as teachers as I improve teaching and learning in my classroom.

IDEAS FOR NEXT STEPS

In her study, Feather Alexander experimented with enlisting students as teachers of their peers in her English classroom. In her final section, Alexander effectively described her own next steps for the improvement of this approach to block-period teaching and learning. She explained, "First, I will give up more control earlier in the course by providing students with activities and options for teaching each other....Giving up more control will help the students to have more responsibility for the course content." Given her intermittent resistance to letting go of the conventional teacher's role, Alexander's first step is a statement of commitment to the value of the approach of students as teachers and a reminder to herself. She concluded, "I plan to use the results of this study to encourage myself to let students become more actively involved (as teachers)."

Alexander continued,

> Although we discussed criteria for good teaching, did role-playing exercises, and discussed how we would approach the teaching aspect of the class, we did not do as good a job clarifying student responsibilities. This created some initial tension and some problems with respect throughout the course. When I ask students to be teachers in the future, we will also clarify the criteria for good listening and appropriate behavior when a group of students is teaching. I hope to devise a way to make students accountable not only for listening to their peers but also for participating fully, perhaps by also giving them a grade in this area, or, better yet, by asking them to assess themselves based on criteria that they themselves have established.

One ongoing weakness in this experiment was the difficulty that some students had in behaving respectfully while their peers were teaching. Here Alexander identifies two interrelated responses to this problem: engaging students in identifying their own responsibilities as learners from each other; and holding students accountable for their behavior in these situations. These activities undertaken together are likely to help students better develop their ability to behave respectfully toward each other in the teacher role.

APPENDIX 4.1 — STUDENT-DEVELOPED RUBRIC FOR ASSESSING TEACHING

A   Excellent; time and effort; creativity; entertaining/fun; open-minded; challenging; willing/able; patient; involvement (by all); cooperation.

B   Above average; lesson not explained completely; time not used up; most students are involved; presentation is good but missing one or two "A" qualities.

C   Average; can be entertaining but not always teaching; not challenging; somewhat clear; lacking originality; lecture most of the time.

D   Below average; not everyone knows what's going on; not clear; some information given; hard to understand; boring; not creative; no class participation; short; no good ideas; dull.

F   Lacking patience and thorough instruction; uninteresting lesson plan; no class activity; not willing to try new approaches and boring the class in the process; the group teaching does not understand the material being taught.

APPENDIX 4.2 — STUDENT SURVEY

Dear Students,

Please respond honestly to the following questions. Your responses will not be graded. The intent is to gather your opinions about activities in this class.

Please respond by circling the number which best corresponds to the statement describing your opinion.

5   Strongly agree
4   Agree
3   Don't know
2   Disagree
1   Strongly disagree

1. Teaching portions of this class are worthwhile

5   4   3   2   1

Why?

2. I like being involved in teaching portions of this class.

5   4   3   2   1

Why?

3. Working together in groups helps me to learn.

5   4   3   2   1

Why?

4. Working together is a good way for us to teach the class.

5   4   3   2   1

Why?

Complete each of the following with your thoughts and opinions. Please explain your answer.

5. In order for me to focus and learn, a teacher's lesson must include...(discuss a helpful learning tool: note taking, group work, hands-on, etc.)

6. Learning is fun when...

5

PERSONAL FITNESS GOAL-SETTING AND STUDENTS' PARTICIPATION IN A PERSONAL FITNESS CLASS

Kristi Noren
Foster High School

Kristi Noren wanted to encourage her less-motivated students in her personal fitness class to become more engaged in the activities of the class and to take more initiative in and responsibility for their exercise participation in class. She believed they lacked personally meaningful fitness goals and sought to involve them in developing their own goals so that they could generate intrinsic motivation for exercise. Using the time made available by a block-period schedule, she gave students more data about their current fitness and strength, helped them to set specific personal goals for improvement, and provided them with individualized fitness workouts.

At the end of the quarter, her data demonstrate important gains in student engagement in exercise and in class grades and, perhaps more importantly, improvements in student attitudes, sense of responsibility for their own fitness, and com-

mitment to exercise. Almost half of the students also demonstrated increased initiative in relation to their exercise
activities.

RESEARCH SETTING

I teach at Foster High School in Tukwila, Washington, a diverse urban and suburban community directly south of Seattle. Foster has about 700 students, about 45% of whom are minority, including about 140 recent immigrants from Somalia and Bosnia. Over 50% of the students receive free or reduced lunch, and about 40% of the school's student population turns over each academic year.

During the 1995-96 school year Foster restructured its day to create an AB schedule, with periods 1, 3, 5 and 2, 4, 6 meeting on alternate days over each two-week period. Periods are 100 minutes, with a 30-minute focus-group meeting each day, between the first and second period of the day.

DESCRIPTION OF THE CLASS

The class I chose to work with for my research project is called personal fitness. Students in this class were in grades 9-12, and about 75% of the students were female.

Personal fitness is cross-credited. Students have a choice of physical education or vocational credit. Most students in this class were seeking the physical education credit to meet a graduation requirement. One-half of the class time consisted of exercise, which was noncompetitive and oriented toward lifestyle fitness activities. On these days, I taught low-impact aerobics, step-aerobics, fitness walking, and weight training. The other class days were spent in the classroom with a curriculum consisting of topics such as self-esteem, body image, healthy cooking (with labs), problem solving and goal setting, anatomy, and health issues such as eating disorders and steroid abuse. My goals for the class were to increase the fitness and health of my students and to motivate them to maintain a fit and healthy lifestyle after leaving the class.

PROBLEM

My concern was for the students who chose not to exercise during fitness activities in the personal fitness class and for other students affected by these peers who provided unhelpful modeling. With the advent of 100-minute periods, the number of students losing participation points had increased because they were choosing to exercise for the first part of the class and then sit for the last portion of the period. This choice had three negative effects on the class:

- It negatively affected the grade and credit of the nonparticipants and limited their opportunity to gain health and fitness benefits from the course.
- It provided a distraction for other students in the class and negatively affected the motivational level of some.
- It limited my effectiveness as a teacher in this class because I was torn between leading group exercises and minimizing the distraction caused by the nonparticipants.

The students who curtailed their participation in exercise part way through the block period did not seem to see the relevance and benefits of exercise and fitness for them, although we had spent some class time listing and discussing such benefits. Their awareness and motivation seemed to be the factor most likely to be affected by my efforts within this classroom, and therefore became the focus of this research.

Other factors that may have influenced some students not to participate fully included these: some students were inappropriately placed in the class; some were lacking the self-concept and maturity to exercise within the view of their peers; and some students were overwhelmed with personal problems.

HYPOTHESIS AND RESPONSE

My hypothesis was that the students who were choosing to drop out of the activities in the middle of the block period lacked motivation for exercise because they lacked personally meaningful fitness goals. My instructional response was to engage them in developing their own goals in this area so that they would generate intrinsic motivation for exercise. My plan for achieving this included these activities:

♦ Dedicate more class time to goal setting activities related to exercise and health.

♦ Increase the scope of student fitness testing to increase data available as goal feedback for students.

♦ During the weight-training unit, provide training programs that are more individually tailored to student fitness goals.

RESEARCH QUESTIONS

My specific research questions were these:

♦ Will increased discussion, guidance, and practice in personal fitness goal-setting increase students' motivation to participate in class exercise?

♦ Does providing additional fitness level data and guidance in personalized fitness goal-setting increase students' motivation to participate in class exercise?

DATA COLLECTION PLAN

My plan for data collection included these elements:

♦ Survey students using a list of 29 attitude and belief statements and a rating scale with 4 selection choices that force a positive or negative response. Students will be identified by student number which will allow matching of pre- and post-surveys and the ability to include only those students in the class for the entire length of the study. (This will remove any bias that might result from the unusually high student turnover rate at Foster.) I can use student assistants to do this matching, which will free me from associating specific students with their survey responses.

♦ Students are currently required to complete a weekly feedback form identifying one success in any part of their lives for the week and the lesson or part of class which "was the best lesson for me in this class last week." I will utilize these forms as a student journal and track the number of successes listed by students that relate to the research. I'll also track the "best lesson" responses, which I will copy weekly onto a list for each student to be analyzed for trends at the conclusion of the research.

♦ I will compare students' exercise participation grades. Students earn a daily exercise score of up to 10 points each workout day. Students who are absent for any reason receive no points; students who are present and do not participate, for any reason, receive 2 points. Students who work to their capacity for the entire period—85 minutes after changing time and attendance/instructions — receive 10 points. Students whose effort or time use are less receive the corresponding percentage of possible points. Students not dressed in exercise-appropriate clothing lose 2 points.

During the weight-training unit, this is measured by a combination of the student's workout card, on which the student lists weights, repetitions, and sets performed, and the teacher's observations as I scan the room every 5 to 10 minutes and note student activity (or lack thereof).

These participation grades will be compiled into class and individual averages before (February/

March) and after (April/May) for the fitness testing and individual goal-planning project. I will
also examine the number of nonparticipants and
partial-participants during each time period. Individual students who have been habitual nonparticipants may be tracked separately as well.

CLASS COMPOSITION

I teach two sections of personal fitness each semester. The
section chosen for this research project was the most challenging, with the highest level of nonparticipation (probably
in the entire eight years I've taught the class). It was also a
small class with only 17 students enrolled, which I anticipated would work well in terms of incorporating the curriculum changes that I had planned.

As the semester progressed, the class became even smaller. The demographics of our district, with a greater than 40%
yearly turnover rate, and the student makeup of the class
both contributed to this reduction. From the beginning of my
project to the end of the semester, I lost two students each to
expulsion, dropping out, and moving. One student was also
severely injured in an accident and under doctor's orders not
to do exercise of any kind. Thus, at the conclusion of the
study period, I had only 10 students whose exercise points
could be compared between both time periods and 11 students whose attitude surveys could be compared.

It is possible that the resulting size of the class influenced
student participation independently of the research factors. I
am sure that the cozy class size at least complemented my efforts to increase the relevance of fitness for students. The class
was not aware that they were the focus of a research project,
but I did tell them that I was doing some different and special
things with them. The group became very cohesive and sup-
portive of each other through the process.

The student not allowed to continue exercising was included in the attitude survey but not the exercise comparison. Two recent immigrants with extremely limited English
vocabulary were not included in the written survey but their
exercise participation was used.

RESEARCH ELEMENTS

FITNESS TESTING

I had the capacity to measure *body composition* (percent lean body mass vs. percent fat body weight) with a hand-held infrared computer or with calipers. Historically, I have allowed students to choose a method so long as we used the same technique each time the individual was measured. For the research group, I used both methods for each student in April and in June. This increased the accuracy of the measurement and gave information about fat distribution for each individual. I considered taking a series of body circumference measurements for each student as well, but was too limited in time.

For *cardiovascular endurance* I did a three-minute step test with immediate and one-, two-, and five-minute pulses to determine the length of time for the heart to return to a rate close to the individual's resting heart rate. The school nurse came into the research class and took a resting pulse rate and blood pressure in April and June for these students so that they could see additional personal proof of their fitness improvement that affects them all day long.

For *flexibility*, students took measurements to evaluate range of motion in eight muscle/joint movements. I felt good about the thoroughness of this test and did not change it for the research group.

Muscle strength and *muscle endurance* were tested respectively with a pushup-till-you-drop test and a one-minute timed abdominal crunch test. For the research group, I continued to do these tests but conducted them as a group instead of with students on their own with partners. With group testing, I hoped to increase accuracy and perhaps add some competition to insure a maximal effort because there is someone next to each student doing the same test at the same time. I also handed out statistical norm rankings for each test that grouped scores into categories of excellent, very good, good, average, and below average. I explained that this information was to help students in their personal fitness goal-setting.

Students also completed a five-day food record to evaluate the interrelationships among food behaviors such as time spent eating, hunger levels, places they eat, who they eat with, emotions and activities while eating, and times and food types. When these behaviors were tallied and evaluated, we discussed healthy habits and ways to make one change at a time toward healthier habits as a component of one's lifestyle. This is a project I have had students do each spring to give them more information for goal-setting.

GOAL-SETTING PROJECT

I have used the Future Homemakers of America's goal-setting project called *Power of One* for several years, with a lot of student success. For the personal fitness class, I have limited student projects to the "Better You" module, which includes many project options related to self-improvement. Students in previous classes have done projects as diverse as improving their chemistry grade, getting along better with a family member, managing their money, getting more sleep, and so on.

I limited the research class to projects that would improve their fitness, including fitness components, food habits, exercise, or reducing stress. For this class, I wanted students not only to learn the goal-setting process and experience success with a personal goal, but also to see more relevance and value in their own fitness habits.

The *Power of One* project included listing concerns, choosing one to improve, writing it as a measurable goal, developing a specific plan to meet the goal and overcome obstacles, and then meeting with an adult mentor in groups of three or four to glean advice and support. After the meeting, students worked on the goal for six weeks and were required to keep documentation daily. For the research class, I was able to keep the group size at two or three. I also decided to weigh the documentation more heavily in the classroom portion of their grades and remind students on at least a weekly basis to enact these projects.

At the end of the six weeks students did some self-evaluation and met again in the small groups to evaluate what they had done and learned, what they would change if doing it over, and how they planned to move forward with the same or a new goal.

INDIVIDUALIZED WORKOUT PROGRAMS

In the third quarter, students had a choice of several lifting programs that I had prewritten, for differing goals and priorities. This was the structure I had used for several years, although I continued to make small changes in the standard programs as new research and information became available.

In April (fourth quarter), I shared a list of my goals for each of my muscle groups (my hobby is amateur drug-free body building) with the research class. I had students make their own personal lists and team up with a partner with similar goals. I then sat down for 20 to 30 minutes with each set of students to write them a special lifting program aligned with their goals and priorities. I had to call some pairs into my focus group to allow enough time to meet with all. I made copies, and this was the program each pair used on exercise days for the remainder of the semester.

Students did decide by majority vote to walk the track on 2 of the 13 exercise days during this period. On walking days, students had to walk four miles for maximum points; they earned fewer points for fewer laps based on a percentage of the four-mile expectation. It was also possible for students who jogged to earn two to four points of extra credit based on mileage.

One of my immigrant students had a leg prosthesis; I dropped the walking days from her grade and wrote her lifting program according to her abilities.

DATA ANALYSIS AND FINDINGS

EXERCISE GRADE COMPARISON

In computing the exercise grades for this study, I made several changes from the framework for grading purposes. I did not count makeup exercise outside of class time or absences in the following percentages since my goal was to affect student participation during class time.

I did, however, count absences for each quarter: there were a total of 18 absences that were not school related among all 11 students for the third quarter, and 23 absences for the fourth quarter. I think the additional fourth quarter absences are typical for this time of year. Ten of the third quarter absences and 7 of those in the fourth quarter (17 in total) belonged to one student who had recurrent bronchitis.

The nonparticipation class totals for each quarter were 10 during the third quarter and 5 during the fourth quarter. This seemed important to me: only five times did a student decide not to participate, half that of the previous quarter!

The following exercise percentage scores are listed in a random order to protect students' identities. The points possible differ due to absences. The percentages in parentheses reflect exercise points with makeup outside of class added in. Students are allowed to bring in one parent/supervisor note per quarter attesting to at least 90 minutes of exercise outside of class for a maximum of 10 points. Beyond this, additional points must be made up, with myself as witness, by special arrangement. During the third quarter, four students took advantage of this opportunity for a total of 45 points. A total of 108 points were earned during the fourth quarter by 6 students, 4 of whom had not done extra credit work earlier.

Exercise Percentage Scores

	Third Quarter		Fourth Quarter	
	Points	Percent (%)	Points	Percent (%)
1	62/60	103 (128)	69/70	99 (112.9)
2	64/100	64	72/100	72 (82)
3	63/100	63	91/110	82 (117)
4	90/110	82 (91)	79/80	99 (111)
5	96/100	96	104/100	104
6	101/110	92	71/90	79 (112)
7	100/110	91 (100)	114/120	95
8	83/110	75	88/100	88
9	104/110	95	91/100	91
10	80/110	73 (82)	88/100	88
11	70/100	70	112/110	102 (111)

The average for the third quarter was 82%. For the fourth quarter it was 91%. Although the total number of exercise days for the third quarter was only 11 and for the fourth quarter only 12, which gives each class a significant impact, I believe that the improvement between quarters was great enough to show a benefit from the research-controlled factors.

Nearly half the students (5 of 11) finished with scores over 100% once the extra credit was added to their fourth quarter points. Three of these students held this distinction even after absences were counted into the actual grades. This amounts to 27% of the class with exercise scores over 100%. It is typical of my other classes to have only about 10% of students reach this score level.

It is interesting to note that one of these excelling students (number one) also counted among the three students whose total scores went down between the quarters. The other students (numbers seven and nine) also completed the fourth quarter with an A grade. There were two students failing (under 70%) in the third quarter and none in the fourth quarter!

Following are the percentage changes between quarters with and without extra credit. Those identified with an asterisk completed with over 100%.

Percentage Changes from Third to Fourth Quarters

Student	Change from 3rd to 4th (%)	Change with extra credit (%)
1	−4.7	−15.4*
2	+8.0	+18.0
3	+19.7	+54.3*
4	+7.9	+20.4*
5	+8.0	NA
6	−12.9	+20.4
7	+4.5	−4.5
8	+13.0	NA

Percentage Changes from Third to Fourth Quarters

Student	Change from 3rd to 4th (%)	Change with extra credit (%)
9	–3.5	NA
10	+15.3	+6.2
11	+32.3	+41.4*

The total increase in percentage points for the class between quarters was 88. This came to an average increase of 8% per student. Including extra credit, the total class increase was 141 percentage points, an average of 13% per student. Since 10% constitutes a grade designation range, this is a significant change in student grades. This improvement was spread among most of the class, with 73% of the students increasing their in-class grade and the same percentage increasing their total grade, including extra credit, from the third to fourth quarters.

Looking at individual student's accomplishments also yields valuable information. Both of the non-English speaking students had increases of about 14% for in-class points. They did not utilize the opportunities for extra credit as much as the other students. Students six and nine experienced personal and friendship-related problems respectively during the fourth quarter. Both confided without my solicitation that these factors were affecting their motivation to workout in class because they were quite worried and upset for a time. Both still earned an A for exercise.

SURVEY RESULT COMPARISON

The survey results are included in Appendix 5.1 (p. 129). In evaluating these results, I found that some statements demonstrate little significant change. The statements relating to attractiveness (numbers 1, 2, and 3) show a slight shift toward a more positive body image, for example, but not enough to be meaningful.

I believe that the timing of the surveys influenced some of the statements relating to stress (4, 5, and 17). The second survey was given during finals week in June, and most students naturally felt a higher level of stress at this time.

The self-evaluations of fitness components (numbers 6 and 15) show interesting information because the surveys were completed shortly after fitness testing in class. Students evaluated their level of cardiovascular endurance and satisfaction with this level as higher in June than in April. There was little change in the responses relating to body composition (lean vs. fat ratio), although several of the students had significant (3–6% of body mass) fat losses. I believe that the additional education and testing done in class shifted student perceptions of what is good, as students began to set higher goals and see their goals as attainable. This relationship was also evident in students' evaluation of being more flexible yet having similar satisfaction rates in June and in April.

The student evaluation of muscle strength and endurance displayed the most outstanding shift in student goals and results. During the weight-training days in May and June, as students' workout effort increased, they made very good gains in strength and in the muscle size and definition that show in the mirror. Daily students would point out how this or that muscle was bigger or showing "cuts" (increased muscle definition). The fitness testing showed significant gains for nearly all students in the pushup and timed crunch tests; in the rare instance that a student did not make a gain, she maintained the same score from April to June. Surprisingly, students rated their levels of muscle strength and endurance and satisfaction much lower at the end of the year.

I believe that most of these students "caught the bug" and wanted to achieve more muscle. In my experience as a personal trainer, most adults typically set much higher weight-training goals once lifting has become a lifestyle habit than they had set prior to their initial weight-training efforts. As a result, my understanding of these lower levels of student satisfaction is that as students gained weight-training experience, they significantly raised their expectations for themselves in this endeavor.

Responses related to enjoying exercise seem to validate this hypothesis. This category of items (numbers 18 and 19) shows the highest degree of positive change in attitude. Only one student claimed not to enjoy lifting, and 8 of the 10 emphatically said, "YES! I enjoy lifting weight," and "YES! I enjoy stretching." Nine of 10 were also emphatic about aerobics and walking, with one "kind-of enjoy it" and none giving negative responses.

Two of the students reported working out harder in class, and one reported using class time more effectively (numbers 21 and 22). No one rated these statements lower in the June survey. There was little change in perception of the value of class workouts (numbers 23 and 24), although two students did not answer number 24 on the second survey.

The expectation of working out in the future (numbers 27–29) also showed minimal change between periods, although 90% claimed "yes" or "kind-of" to expecting to be exercising both next year and 10 years in the future. All had this expectation for summer.

STUDENT FEEDBACK RESPONSES

On the weekly feedback forms, students were required to list at least one success for the week and to complete this statement: "The best lesson for me this week in this class was...." Optional questions asked if anything was bothering them, if they would like help with something, and if they have exercised outside of class during the week. There was also space for other comments. I always commented in writing on these forms and nearly always returned them within one week.

In March and April, an average of 50% of students reported exercising outside of class. From April 30th on, all of the English-speaking students reported at least some exercise during each week outside of class. I was thrilled to see them incorporate more exercise into their lifestyles!

The following are illustrative student comments from their completion of the "best lesson" statement. I have listed the dates and added student numbers from the exercise point chart for cross-referencing.

Comments related to the student's goal project:

Student	Date	Comment
4	3/25	I have something to look forward to at the end of the year. My health goal.
11	4/16	...eating right. I'm trying to eat healthy and right.
11	4/30	...things I can eat and still keep my abs. I'm trying to lose some of that (fat) on my abs.
2	4/30	...making (a) healthy breakfast. I am often in a hurry and I just grab anything to eat. Now I prepare my breakfast the day before and eat it in the morning.
1	4/30	...I have started getting up early in the morning to exercise before I get ready for school.
5	5/6	...a paper to help you with your daily planner to keep you on schedule.
6	5/6	...to stay fit and strong. I want to be healthy and beautiful not lazy.
7	5/6	...starting my new workout program. It gives me a chance to workout on the body parts I need help with.
7	5/14	...being able to start my first day of my new schedule, because it gives me a chance to work on improvement on my body.

Comments related to workouts:

Student	Date	Comment
4	3/11	...working in the weight room. I'm trying to improve my appearance.
9	4/1	...It felt good working out. I was really stressed out!
10	4/16	...Every class is good for me. It is (a) good class.
1	4/16	...always, on how to lift weights.
9	4/16	...It felt good to workout. I needed it after spring break.
4	4/16	...workout. My muscle is starting to tone up.
3	4/16	...the workout day. I see and most definitely feel improvement.
9	4/22	...I really feel good. I'm working out more often and I feel a lot healthier.
3	4/22	...the workout. It shows definition (in muscles). I like that.
6	4/22	...to stay in shape. It's good to feel strong, healthy, and young.
9	4/22	...exercise. I like it.
10	4/30	...every class (is) good for me. I like exercise.
3	4/30	...the weight lifting. It's helping me to get physically fit.
9	5/6	...on Monday I liked working out. I needed to because I feel better when I workout!
3	5/6	...to be fit. It's very good for the body.
10	5/6	...exercise. I like that.
2	5/14	...planning my workout routine correctly because that's the correct way to workout.

Some comments from other student writing:

Student	Date	Comment
5	June	I have so far stuck to my exercise program and even on busy days I still workout. I feel healthier than ever and less stressful. I want to stick to my exercise routine so that is a daily part of my life.
11	June	...my abs, it's smaller. Not only I notice it, but my family and friends. I don't want to stop working on my abs....I am able to zip up the back of my dress because I couldn't do that before....I eat less junk food and more healthy food....
1	June	Out of everything, I think my cardio endurance has improved the most. I can walk up a small hill without being totally out of breath and I can walk 15 to 17 laps (3¾ to 4¼ miles!) without being really tired.
7	June	Things that have bothered me were not getting enough exercise. Now I see improvement. Now I can walk, run or do any kind of exercise (outside of class) 3–4 times a week without missing a day. The activities outside of class for me have been great....Some new exercises I would like to try (are) going to a workout gym, and working in an aerobic class.

Student's verbal comments in class also showed an increased understanding of the benefits of exercise to them as individuals. They referred not only to how they physically looked, but to how they felt both physically and emotionally. Students also often expressed pride in their accomplishments, in their goals, and in class. For some students successes at school are not routine. I hope they are able to translate this successful self-image to other aspects of school and to life in general.

CONCLUSION

I am very satisfied with the results of this project. The students' grades increased, their motivation and participation improved, and we all enjoyed coming to class and working together. I certainly benefited from the improved atmosphere in the group as much as the students themselves did.

Because part of the class' success undoubtedly lies in the small size of the research group, it will be a challenge to continue this level of personalization in fitness testing and programming in future classes of 30 or more students. I believe the innovations to be valuable enough, however, to supplant some other pieces of curriculum content. I am looking forward to developing creative ways to use the lessons of this research effectively in larger classes and thus positively influence more students' lives.

IDEAS FOR NEXT STEPS

In her study, Kristi Noren demonstrated that by helping her students to articulate personally meaningful exercise goals and by providing them with elaborate feedback about their current fitness and strength, she could encourage them both to exercise more in class and outside of class and to improve their attitudes and motivation in relation to fitness.

As Noren notes,

> Because part of the class' success undoubtedly lies in the small size of the research group, it will be a challenge to continue this level of personalization in fitness testing and programming in future classes of 30 or more students. I believe the innovations to be valuable enough, however, to supplant some other pieces of curriculum content. I am looking forward to developing creative ways that I can use the lessons of this research effectively in larger classes and thus positively influence more students' lives.

Noren understands clearly that the power of her experiment lies in her ability to personalize her transactions with students: personalized fitness goals, personalized fitness data, and personalized workout programs. Her challenge is to maintain this quality of interaction with students in a class two or three times as large. She can't do this in exactly the same way because she is only one person. But she can create structures in her classroom that develop the qualities of personalization that she achieved in this study to at least some significant degree.

In this study, Noren used pairs for some purposes. But with a larger class she'd need to organize students into trios. She could talk with the class about fitness goals and perhaps model the goal-setting process with a volunteer student or two. She could also engage the class in developing a rubric for describing what constitutes an appropriate set of fitness goals. Once the rubric was completed, she could set the trios of students to work at identifying specific goals for each member. As they worked, she could move around the room to touch base with each trio, provide direction and input, answer questions, redirect students, and so on. Each student would hand in her or his completed goals to Noren, and she could respond to them in writing as a general practice, with the option of conversations with some students as needed.

Noren could also work with the same or different trios both to provide more data to students about their current fitness status and to provide students with more individually tailored workout programs. For example, she could group students with similar training needs into trios and then generate a training program for each group. While there is no way that Noren can recreate all of the familiarity and personal availability that she established in her small research class with a class of 30 students, she can certainly apply the principles that she developed in her action research—increased fitness testing, more feedback to students about fitness, greater emphasis on fitness goal-setting, provision of a personalized training program, and personalization as a theme throughout the class—to larger class sizes.

APPENDIX 5.1 — SURVEY RESULTS

The first number under each response indicates the number of students choosing that response at the end of the third quarter prior to the application of research controlled factors. The second number indicates responses at the end of the fourth quarter. Ten students completed both surveys; however, some skipped a question or two, so not all responses add up to 10.

		Yes	*"Kind-of"*	*Not Really*	*No*
1.	I think I am attractive.	4/6	4/3	2/0	0/1
2.	My peers see me	4/6	5/4	1/0	
3.	The opposite gender see me as attractive.	4/5	5/4	1/1	
4.	I sleep well at night.	3/3	4/2	2/3	1/2
5.	I am usually well-rested.	2/0	3/6	3/1	2/3
6.	I have good cardiovascular endurance.	2/2	4/6	4/1	0/1
7.	I am satisfied with my level of cardio endurance	1/3	3/4	5/2	3/1
8.	I have a good body composition (body fat ratio).	2/3	4/3	1/1	3/3
9.	I am satisfied with my body composition.	1/1	4/4	0/1	4/4
10.	I have good flexibility.	4/6	4/2	1/1	1/1
11.	I am satisfied with my level of flexibility.	3/3	4/4	1/2	2/1
12.	I have good muscle strength.	5/1	1/3	2/6	2/0
13.	I am satisfied with my muscle strength.	4/1	2/4	2/4	2/1
14.	I have good muscle endurance.	3/4	4/2	2/4	1/0

	Yes	"Kind-of"	Not Really	No
15. I am satisfied with my muscle endurance.	4/2	1/2	3/5	1/1
16. I have good posture.	4/5	4/4	1/0	1/1
17. I have too much stress.	4/6	4/2	1/2	1/0
18. I enjoy lifting weight.	4/8	3/1	2/0	0/1
19. I enjoy stretching.	5/8	4/1	1/1	
20. I enjoy aerobics and walking.	7/9	3/1		
21. I work out to my full ability in class.	4/5	4/5	2/0	
22. I use class exercise time effectively.	4/5	6/5		
23. I believe class workouts will improve my fitness level.	9/9	1/1		
24. I believe class workouts will improve my overall health.	8/6	1/2	1/1	0/1
25. I want to be more physically fit.	9/9		1/1	
26. I have a plan to improve my fitness.	6/7	2/0	2/3	
27. I expect to be working out regularly this summer.	8/7	2/3		
28. I expect I will be working-out regularly next year.	7/7	2/2	1/1	
29. I expect I will be working-out regularly 10 years from now.	5/6	3/3	1/1	

6

THE DEPTH VS. COVERAGE TRADEOFF: PROJECT ASSESSMENT IN U.S. HISTORY BLOCK PERIODS

Chris Drape
Lindbergh High School

Chris Drape wanted to explore the depth-of-study-versus-coverage dilemma in United States history. He wrote in his research journal: "I want to know if by diving in deeply and complexly—having students create something unique, original, and involved—I can alter their own perceptions of themselves as actors vs. receivers in this class...and whether or not that matters." Could he help his students begin to see history as a subject of both interest and importance in their own lives?

A block-period schedule allowed Drape to involve his students in a significant research study that required them to take information from class lectures, poetry, primary source documents, and interviews, analyze the information, and form their own conclusions about the Vietnam War experience and its impact on American society. Students enacted much of the project in class through a workshop approach. "This project in its entirety was the most involved piece of independent and original historical work most of these students had done in their school careers," Drape noted.

Is such a project worth this concentration of time and energy, particularly in light of the resulting loss of coverage of other topics that results?

Drape's data suggest the answer is yes, with some appropriate cautions. "The project engaged students meaningfully in first-hand historical work. They became the 'doers' instead of the 'receivers.'...[T]here are some subtle yet important messages about the importance of giving students more power in their study of history if we seek their meaningful involvement in this enterprise."

INTRODUCTION

I am a U.S. history teacher and I did not cover World War II in class this year. This confession communicates the ongoing dilemma I face and my motivation to pursue this action-research project. As a high school history teacher, I constantly struggle with the depth-versus-coverage issue. I have a U.S. history textbook with 36 chapters. There are 36 weeks in the school year. It doesn't take a rocket scientist to see a connection, but it would take a great many rocket scientists to figure out how to meaningfully and with retention take students through those 36 chapters, 1 per week.

My first 2 years of teaching were in a traditional 6-period day (55-minute classes), and in that context I struggled with the question of what to leave out. I am now in my second year of teaching in the block-period schedule and am motivated to address that question even more critically. In the block period, I believe I involve students in more creative and student-directed work than I could in the six-period day. I engage them more effectively, but this amplifies the depth-versus-coverage challenge. We are covering content more thoroughly and meaningfully, but we are also covering less material. Is that legitimate?

QUESTION

Simply put, my research questions are these:

♦ Given that block periods already tend to sacrifice coverage for depth, are student projects that require significant blocks of time productive and meaningful ways to use the block period?

◆ What do students gain through projects and depth, and are these gains an acceptable trade-off for less coverage?

Within the block period I am confronted even more regularly with the "what to leave out" question. This is a very critical question for me as a history teacher because I have the power to shape attitudes and perceptions by what I choose to cover or to leave out. I trust myself with that task, but I am more concerned about whether my students know ideas and pertinent information well. Can they think and speak meaningfully about the topics we cover? Can they apply the structure of this learning to new situations? I cannot cover everything important about U.S. history in the short 36 weeks I have with my students, but I can teach about key ideas, issues, and themes in such a way that they develop their skills as historians and gain judgment. As the historian Paul Gagnon said:

> People asked then, as they ask now, Why history, and why so much of it?...The answer goes back to judgment, which requires more than knowing where the tools of self-government are and how to wield them. Judgment implies nothing less than wisdom—an even bigger word—about human nature and society. It takes a sense of the tragic and of the comic to make a citizen of good judgment.... Tragedy, comedy, paradox, and beauty are not the ordinary stuff of even the best courses in civics and government. But history, along with biography and literature, if they are well taught, cannot help but convey them.[1]

My goal is to tell the story of U. S. history well. Too many of my students come to my class not caring much about anything. I want them to care, and by telling the story well, by helping them to tell the story themselves, I believe I can accomplish this task. As I wrote in my first journal entry for this

---

1. Paul Gagnon, "Why Study History?," *The Atlantic Monthly,* November 1988, pp. 43–66.

study, "What do I want to learn? I want to know if by diving in deeply and complexly—having students create something unique, original and involved—I can alter their own perceptions of themselves as actors vs. receivers in this class...and whether or not that matters."

CONTEXT

I teach at Lindbergh High School in Renton, Washington, a working-class and middle-class suburb of Seattle and home to the Boeing Corporation. Our school of approximately 1,220 students (grades 9–12) is growing in diversity but is still primarily white (68% Caucasian, 17% Asian American, 10% African American, 3% Latino, and 2% Native American). This year I taught four sections of U.S. history, the eleventh grade social studies requirement, and one section of American studies, an integrated U.S. history-American literature class, team-taught with a language arts teacher. I focused on two of my U.S. history classes for this research. Because we do not offer honors classes within the social studies department, the students in these two classes represent the full range of the Lindbergh student population. In 1995 we, as a staff, decided to move to a block period schedule as follows:

1st/4th Period:	7:20–9:04
Advisory:	9:09–9:34
2nd/5th Period:	9:44–11:27
3rd/6th Period:	12:17–2:00

Periods one, two, and three meet on Mondays and Thursdays. Periods four, five, and six meet on Tuesdays and Fridays. Wednesdays follow our former 6-period schedule with 55-minute classes.

DATA COLLECTION PLAN

I feel the need to return to the opening statement for a little justification. The statement is not entirely true. We did cover World War II but in a larger, thematic unit on war that focused on Vietnam as a case study. I created a project focusing on the Vietnam experience to use as the raw material for my research. The project was structured around the belief, explained above, that one of my goals as a history teacher is to help students develop the skills of an historian. To this end, the project required students to take information we covered (from class lecture, to poetry, to primary documents, to interviews), analyze it, and form their own conclusions about the Vietnam experience and its impact on American society. The general project assignment (I created more detailed, followup guides for each of the components) is Appendix 6.1 (p. 149). The project had four major components:

- ♦ Interview

  Students had to identify and interview someone who lived through the Vietnam era and could comment meaningfully about his or her experience.

- ♦ Primary Source Analysis

  Students chose one primary source document related to the Vietnam experience from four options, and they interpreted the document in terms of what it had to say about the experience.

- ♦ Poem Analysis

  Students chose one poem related to the Vietnam experience from three options and analyzed it in terms of what it communicated about the impact of the experience on the U.S.

- ♦ Primary Source–Poem Comparison

  Students compared and contrasted the messages of the document and the poem.

We used a significant amount of class time to work through the various components of the project. I wanted students to wrestle this out, but I also wanted them to do it in a context in which they could be successful. The block period time frame allowed a more focused workshop approach. We discussed and analyzed examples of primary documents and poems; then students had time to work independently. After completing the four components, students compiled their work, created a cover with a title and visual, and wrote an introduction in which they discussed their overall interpretation of the impact the Vietnam experience had on American society. Though students had conducted each of the various components of this project earlier in the year, this project in its entirety was the most involved piece of independent and original historical work most of these students had done in their school careers. The project was my opportunity to catch them at work and see what they thought about in-depth historical analysis. While they studied Vietnam, I studied them.

My data collection plan had five components:

♦ Student Journals

Students responded to three in-class prompts (each a set of questions) related to the project (see Appendix 6.2, p. 151, for journal questions and results). Through the student journals I hoped to:

- gauge student attitudes toward history;
- gauge student reactions to the project, to the process of becoming historians; and
- gauge student reactions to what they produced.

All of this was done with the assumption that wrestling with meaningful content in a deep way and developing the skills of the historian are worthwhile tasks for high school students. The question is whether the payoff is significant enough, given the amount of time such a project takes and the resulting loss of coverage of other topics.

♦ Student Focus Group

I conducted a focus group discussion with four students to gain further insight into their reactions to the project and to the depth-versus-coverage question (see Appendix 6.3, p. 155, for these questions). The goal of this component was to allow me to go beyond the scope of journal responses, to ask open-ended questions, and to be able to follow up on them with additional questions.

◆ Teacher Focus Group

I conducted a focus group discussion with five other teachers from Lindbergh regarding their thoughts on depth versus coverage and on the use of time in the block period (see Appendix 6.4, p. 156, for these questions). I wanted to explore how their thoughts compared to mine. How do other history teachers come to terms with the depth-versus-coverage issue, especially in block periods?

◆ Parent Input

Parents responded to a four-question survey that was sent home at the end of the project (see Appendix 6.5, p. 157, for parent questionnaire and results). I wanted to get a sense of the parents' perspectives. Did they notice differences in their child's work and attitudes? Given what they saw in this project, what did they think about the legitimacy of in-depth projects?

◆ Teacher Journal

I kept an ongoing journal of my thoughts and reactions to the project as we went along. This allowed me to note general observations about the project and the process as well as to document specific discoveries along the way.

DATA ANALYSIS

STUDENTS

As mentioned earlier, input from students came in three forms: the projects themselves, the students' journals, and the focus group.

THE PROJECT

One of the measurements that I used to determine the legitimacy of in-depth project work was the quality of the work the students produced. Such evaluation is a relatively subjective process, but I tried to objectify it enough to draw meaningful conclusions. The project was completed during the fourth quarter. I compared the student scores on the project with their overall third-quarter grades. This gave me a general benchmark of student performance (third-quarter grade) and allowed me to see if their work on the project exhibited any significant differences. Overall I was very impressed with the quality of work the students produced, and the grade comparisons illustrate a significant difference.

- ♦ Period One
  3rd quarter average: 73%
  Project average: 81%

- ♦ Period Two
  3rd quarter average: 85%
  Project average: 93%

The student grades on the project were, on average, 8% higher than the average third-quarter grade. This is almost a full grade. I graded the projects rigorously, and the high scores listed are legitimate. It is hard to decide on any single factor that explains the significantly higher project scores, but clearly the students were engaged enough to work hard and well. I believe that a real factor is that the project engaged students meaningfully in first-hand historical work. They became the doers instead of the receivers and, as we will see later, that was a significant factor for them.

STUDENT JOURNALS

My bias in teaching history is to get the students to move beyond the textbook, to get at history in meaningful and interesting ways, and to be historians themselves. The first journal prompts were designed to elicit responses that communicate students' general attitudes toward history. It became clear that they do not come to class with much prior engagement. I asked them what they liked and did not like about history. Generally, what they liked was learning new information (12 of 45 total responses [27%]; Note: not all students responded to all questions, so numbers vary). What they did not like fell into four main areas that are related. Ten students (22%) did not like "memorizing dates"; 10 (22%) did not like "repetition/irrelevant things"; 9 (20%) commented that history was generally "boring"; and 8 students (18%) were not excited about "lectures and notes." These are the voices of students disconnected from the history they are supposed to be learning. Granted, it is not my job to entertain students, but it is my job to engage them.

The second journal focused on student attitudes toward the project itself. They answered these questions approximately a week after the project had been introduced, so they had not yet thoroughly involved themselves in the project. Sixteen of 43 (37%) students commented that the subject of the project was interesting, while 10 (23%) were interested in the project itself. Eleven (25%) were concerned with the workload and amount of time the project would take. (For about one-third of my students this project came at the same time as the junior research paper completed in their language arts class.) Six students (14%) responded that this was just another school project. The numbers give an overall sense of attitudes, but direct quotes from some students better communicate these attitudes. One quote represented the positive attitudes expressed in the journals: "I'm kind of excited to finally experience history in person, instead of just reading about it." A second quote identified the concerns some students experience in response to such a focused project: "I don't like how we are going to be focusing on only this event for such a long time."

An additional question regarding the project involves students' expectations. Fifteen of 43 (35%) students responded that they looked forward to "learning more." But a significant 19 students (44%) said that they were looking forward to the interview: "I look forward to [getting] to know about the war [from] a person that was actually in it by interviewing them, to get what we didn't learn in books." Another added, "…[W]e will learn about what was going on, in a regular person's point of view." I was pleasantly surprised by how many students were thoughtfully anticipating the interviews.

The third journal, the project evaluation, was done in two parts and was designed to gauge student perceptions of their own product and its impact on them. In the end, though they had not all initially been excited about the project, 37 of 42 students (88%) said that it was a valuable experience: "…[I]t gave us a chance to learn something on our own—and we *had* to learn something in order to do it, so we really had to get our hand into what we've been studying." Another responded, "I think this project was a more valuable experience because we got to find out the information for ourselves instead of having to be fed it." Another student elaborated on this idea:

> When I cover something in school, it is really short and I don't care. We quickly move on to something else to cover in a brief amount of time, and I usually forget about all of that stuff. This project made me go deeper, and it gave me a chance to get interested in the subject rather than breeze through it, giving me no depth and making it "just another event in history."

When asked what they liked about the project, 17 students (40%) said the interview and 12 others (29%) said "getting beyond the facts/learning about personal experiences." "I liked the interview. It made the Vietnam War more than just writing in a book or a subject in a class, I could really see its reality." These quotes speak to the value of taking the time to explore an historical topic in depth.

When asked how they felt about what they had produced, 19 of 39 students (49%) said they felt good or were proud of what they had created; another 8 (21%) said they were satisfied, though in retrospect they realized that they could have worked harder and done better. I also asked if such a project changed their view of their own capabilities. Twenty-five (64%) said no (most commented that they were already aware of their capabilities), but 13 (33%) said the project did affect their views of their own abilities: "I like the fact that this showed me that I am able and competent to complete a thorough job on a task. It may make it easier for similar assignments to come." This number is significant if such a change has a lasting impact on how these students work in the future. For this reason alone, I would argue the clear value of this kind of extended project. A solid majority of 29 students (74%) said that the project had a positive impact on their learning of the content: "…[I]t helped me discover for myself the answers to some of the confusing parts, instead of being told by a teacher." "It is another way of learning which is more helpful and meaningful than book work." Finally, when asked how this affected their ability to play the role of an historian, 11 students (28%) said it strengthened their ability while 10 (26%) said that it did not affect their ability.

Though there are no dramatic discoveries here, there are some subtle yet important messages about the importance of giving students more power in their study of history if we seek their meaningful involvement in this enterprise.

STUDENT FOCUS GROUP

In my discussion with the four students (two male, two female, and representing a range in ethnicity, academic ability, and motivation), they elaborated on the themes that were identified in the journals. There was consensus among them that there needs to be a variety in the use of time in block periods. They also agreed that it seems that less material is covered in block periods as compared to the six-period schedule, which these students experienced as freshmen. They believed that this "less material" is covered better in lab classes, and they emphasized the need to use time efficiently. Two students who were in advanced classes thought that it was a problem that they did not get to more material (they were speaking of their advanced language arts class). All of the students were in general agreement that teachers stay focused better in the shorter (55-minute) class periods.

In regard to our specific U.S. history class, all agreed that they would prefer a few topics in more detail. Comments were made about the repetitive coverage of events year-to-year in the history classes the students take (the "we're sick of hearing about the Pilgrims" syndrome). This is a significant concern to heed. If students are tuning out before we even get started, I will certainly have problems engaging them.

Finally, there was consensus on the fact that students work harder on projects, but if given the choice, most would choose taking tests because they see that as easier. "A test is memorization, not analysis. In a project I'm doing and learning…I remember the stuff. I wish it was just a test, but that's because I didn't want to work." They agreed that they felt better about their accomplishments after projects than tests.

Such feedback, though anecdotal in nature, provides insight into the positive aspects of depth. The quality of the projects and the student feedback support my assertion that such projects are meaningful and important ways to engage students in the content. Yet the drawback of less coverage remains. Overall, the positive student responses to the project support the trade-off, but there clearly needs to be a balance.

FACULTY

Because I have been teaching for only four years, I thought it important to broaden the discussion of depth versus coverage to include a wider range of faculty experience. I led a focus group discussion with five other teachers from Lindbergh, four from the social studies department and one from language arts (with whom I team teach the American studies class). The teaching experience of the group ranged from 1 year to 25 years. The question I posed as the general context for our discussion was how to strike a balance between depth and coverage in block periods, with a focus on U.S. history content. There was, not surprisingly, consensus that less material is covered in the block period as compared to 55-minute periods; several reasons were given for this difference:

◆ In shorter periods, there is a greater tendency to tell students rather than help them discover information.

◆ The time structure in block periods allows for more focus on process.

◆ With the luxury of more concentrated time blocks, teachers are more willing to pursue tangents (or let the pursuit last longer).

An interesting note on time use was the observation by one teacher that he spends the same number of days on a given unit in the block-period schedule than he did in the 55-minute period schedule. This means that he essentially spends twice as much time on each unit as he did in the short periods. He explained that he covers the same material but from more perspectives and in different ways. This idea led us to the question of the definition of *depth*, which proved slippery. Does depth mean knowing more about fewer topics, spending more time on fewer topics, or focusing more on process than content? We did not reach agreement on a definition. We did agree, however, that a benefit of this slower approach is that although more time spent does not guarantee greater depth of knowledge for every individual student, as one focuses more on process and on approaching material from a greater array of angles, one addresses a greater variety of learning styles and, therefore, reaches more students more meaningfully. This depth allows for helping students learn the tools of the historian's trade, process over facts. But the issue of depth demands continued exploration and reflection. Depth can also be illusory, and we can fool ourselves that more time devoted to a topic necessarily means more knowledge. Though this is not always the case, the possible costs of devoting more class time to a topic without achieving more student knowledge can be offset by more effective engagement of a wider range of students through the use of more diverse learning activities.

PARENTS

As I began this research I decided that I wanted to gain some insight into the parent perspective on what their children were doing in my classroom. This data source is limited, because not all parents are connected to their child's schoolwork in high school. Nonetheless parents can provide an important third perspective on some of the questions, particularly when we take the time to ask for their comments.

When we began the project, I sent a letter home (see Appendix 6.6, p. 158) to parents explaining what we were undertaking and letting them know that I would be sending home a questionnaire for them at the end of the project. Students had to turn this questionnaire in with their final project. I received back 31 (of a possible 46) questionnaires. My goal in surveying the parents was to get their input on the depth-versus-coverage issue, as well as their impressions and reactions to their children's creations.

When asked whether they believed this project was a valuable experience, 26 of 31 parents (84%) responded positively. The actual responses were enlightening and echoed the thoughts of students regarding the significance of such a project. "It actually means more to find out first-hand by people actually affected by it," one parent explained. In response to the question of what changes in attitude took place during the project, one parent said, "It was just 'another' assignment at first. But it was brought closer to home (and heart) by actually digging in and finding out some more 'personal' aspects, actually true stories." Another commented on her son's perspective: "He was very doubtful of the project, on how hard it was. Seeing the change in his attitude was overwhelming." These quotes point to this project as a way to draw students in, oftentimes sparking interest in those students who are generally disconnected from such dry topics as history.

In response to the final question, 29 parents (94%) said that trading some coverage for the kind of depth this project exhibited was acceptable. I was pleasantly surprised by such consensus. One parent commented, "I think it is better to really study one subject than skim over a bunch of things." Another added, "I think this is what schools should be doing with history subjects." Significantly, many of the comments that related to the importance of such a project referred to the impact of the interviews on the students. This statement was typical: "...[A]s she read and studied she started to take an interest. Her interview made the war more real to her." One parent even commented regarding the interview, "It was good for me to open up about my experiences." Overall the parent responses supported the idea that depth leads to engagement and more worthwhile activities in the classroom.

CONCLUSIONS AND ACTION PLAN

The most rewarding aspect for me in this whole process was the projects the students created. On their own they lend credence to the value of in-depth study. I was impressed across the board by the quality and thoughtfulness of their projects. This held for the motivated students who generally do well, as well as for a substantial number of underachievers, who rose to the occasion and met the challenge of this project. From the journals I was able to hear in detail about the impact this project had, an impact that I hope will linger and, ideally, could be built upon in the future. One student commented, "I like [the project] because it gave me the chance to do research It gave me reasons for the war." Another said, "Instead of just reading what somebody else wrote, we were able to get the information on our own and talk to people first-hand." These kinds of reaction suggest that the students have developed new ways of thinking about their role in a U.S. history class. Though all students might not have left feeling empowered to be full-fledged historians, I believe they are different because of the project. In a coverage approach, there is no opportunity to give students the latitude to explore and to create, the chance to get interested and hooked—and this is key to teaching history well to adolescents.

Most of the feedback, from students, teachers, and parents, supported the idea of trading some coverage for depth and exploring content through projects such as the one outlined here. But there are some cautions I have identified in this research as well. I cannot, and should not, do such an in-depth project with every unit. These are large undertakings and I will drain both myself and my students if I overload us. And, as the students commented in the focus group, they desire variety. Even a good project, repeated too often, gets old.

A second caution came from the teacher focus group. In a U.S. history survey class one must choose the themes and topics of such projects wisely. In retrospect, my focus on Vietnam may have been overly narrow. Though I tied it into our larger theme of war, I must be careful to choose topics that are broad enough that students are able to translate what they get from the project to larger issues and themes of U.S. history.

This research covers a range of issues related to teaching and learning in block periods, but they all relate to the freedom and opportunity a teacher has with larger blocks of time. This freedom and opportunity allow for more depth and creativity in what I have students do, but there is a caution. There needs to be balance and variety in any approach.

Perhaps the clearest message I received from the research is the value of interviewing my students and treating their analyses of our classroom with respect. This component of the project clearly impacted students and parents the most. While not all topics and time frames lend themselves to interviews, I can take better advantage of this process than I currently do. Additionally, given the feedback from the parent questionnaires, I would like to bring more of this reflective, interactive, data-generating aspect to student work. It is important for both the students and the parents, and it provides me with valuable insight into the effects and outcomes of my teaching.

History is a story that must be told well. I believe that projects such as the one I have described, projects that not only go behind the scenes of the textbook version but that also include students in the telling, are significant and meaningful ways to engage students in learning about U.S. history. My challenge is to find a balance between depth and coverage and to identify appropriate themes and topics for depth. In light of this research project, it is clear to me that taking advantage of the time structure in block periods to pursue in-depth projects has value.

IDEAS FOR NEXT STEPS

In his study, Chris Drape explored the value of involving students in an in-depth study in his U.S. history classroom. In his final section, Drape identifies several ideas for improvement of this kind of student project and that while the research project was successful, it is not appropriate or practical for students to conduct this type of project in every unit. Given this understanding, a task for Drape is to reflect upon his year-long U.S. history curriculum and decide how many in-depth projects he would like his students to complete and in which units these projects should reside.

Drape notes,

> In a U.S. history survey class, one must choose the themes and topics of such projects wisely. In retrospect, my focus on Vietnam may have been overly narrow. Though I tied it into our larger theme of war, I must be careful to choose topics that are broad enough that students are able to translate what they get from the project to larger issues and themes of U.S. history.

In this comment, Drape articulates some initial criteria for devising and defining worthwhile projects of this sort. Another task of refinement for him includes both the further development of these criteria for a "good in-depth project" and the application of such criteria in the development of the various specific projects in his curriculum.

Drape highlights "the value of interviewing my students and treating their analyses of our classroom with respect." This recognition of the value of gathering formal, structured feedback from his students about their experience of his classroom can lead Drape to envision this kind of data collection as a central activity in his effort to improve his teaching practice.

Finally, Drape might want to view his collection of data from parents in a similar light. It is likely that his involvement of parents in this study resulted in the parents' increasing the amount of attention they gave to their child's school work for this class and that this increase in attention had positive outcomes for the student and the parent. If this assumption is accurate, it suggests the Drape might want to make parent involvement a regular element in at least some of these in-depth projects.

APPENDIX 6.1 — PROJECT

Vietnam Experience: The Impact of the War
Due Mon./Tue. May 12/13
150 points

We will explore the U.S. experience in Vietnam in detail by each undertaking a project that will shed light on a personal experience with the war. Our goal is to understand the impact the war had on the U.S. There will be multiple components to the project that will be compiled into the final product.

We will expand and work on each of these components in class, but there will also be a significant amount of out-of-class time that you will need to commit to the project.

COMPONENTS

1. *Interview:* You will talk to someone about his/her experience with the war and write an essay-form report of what you learn in the interview. We will talk about this more in class.

   Proposal due: April 21/22
        —who you will interview
        —your prepared questions
   Final write-up due with final project

2. *Primary Source Analysis:* You will read and analyze a primary source related to the U.S. experience in Vietnam. We will explore options and look at documents in class.

   Draft due: April 24/25
   Final due with final project

3. *Poem Response:* You will read and analyze a poem written in response to the war. The four choices available are in your reading packet. You can also propose alternatives.

   Draft due: April 28/29
   Final due with final project

4. *Poem/Source Comparison:* You will compare and contrast the ideas of your primary source and your poem.

Due with final project

COMPILATION AND GRADING

10 points	Cover/Title Page (includes appropriate title and visual).
30	Introduction (1–2-page essay setting the stage, communicating what you have discovered through our look at the war and the four steps listed above). The four sections listed above:
35	Interview writeup;
20	Primary document analysis;
20	Poem analysis;
15	Comparison.
5	Parent questionnaire.
15	Mechanics (grammar, punctuation, typed...): The final project should be typed and well organized. We are creating quality products here.

EXTRA CREDIT:

Do a book or movie review that relates to the Vietnam experience. You must OK this with Mr. Drape *BEFORE* you read or watch.

APPENDIX 6.2 — STUDENT JOURNAL QUESTIONS

JOURNAL #1 (You and History)
45 total student responses

1. What do you like about history? Why?
   Learning new things: 12
   Discovering lessons learned/mistakes made: 7
   Seeing choices/decision: 3

2. What don't you like about history? Why?
   Memorizing dates: 10
   Repetition/irrelevant things: 10
   It's boring: 9
   Lectures/taking notes: 8
   Reading/answering questions: 2
   Long projects: 1

3. What does an historian do?
   (All answers essentially said teach others about the past)

4. What is the difference between you and an historian?
   Historian knows more: 17
   I don't teach others: 13
   Historian gathers information: 6
   We do this (project) because it's required: 5
   Not much: 2
   Historian shares his own opinion: 1

JOURNAL #2 (You and the Project)
43 total student responses

1. What is your attitude toward this project and why?
   (interested in it…dreading it…explain)
   Subject is interesting: 16
   Concerned about workload/time: 11
   Project is interesting: 10
   It's just another project: 6
   Don't really care: 5
   Not interested in subject: 3
   Hard: 1

2. What do you look forward to in this project?
    Talking to parents/interviewing people: 19
    Learning more: 15
    Poem response: 3
    Nothing: 3
    Have it over with: 2
    Expressing my own views: 1

3. What do you want to get out of this project?
    Learn more: 33
    Finish/good grade: 7
    Hear personal stories: 2
    Know parents better: 1

PROJECT EVALUATION #1
42 total student responses

1. In relation to the other kinds of assignments you have in school, do you think this project was a valuable experience? Explain.
    Yes: 37
    No: 5

2. What did you like about the project? Why?
    The interview: 17
    Learning about people's experiences: 12
    Cover page/visual: 3
    Wasn't just regurgitating information: 1
    Poems: 1
    Scope of project: 1
    Learning new stuff: 1
    Choices: 1
    Nothing: 1

3. What didn't you like about the project? Why?
    Timing: 6
    Comparisons: 5
    Essays: 5
    Typing: 3
    Hard to talk about: 3
    Hard to find interviewee: 3
    Poems: 2
    Dragged on: 2

Only dealt with personal experiences: 2
Primary analysis: 1
Hard: 1
Everything: 1

4. How did this project compare to work in other classes (history or not...)?
> harder, easier, more fun, less fun...
Harder (essays, time-consuming): 12
Easier (not book work, added own opinion): 10
More fun: 9
More interesting: 5
Less fun: 4
Same: 1
More complicated: 1

PROJECT EVALUATION #2
39 total student responses

1. How do you feel about what you have produced? Explain.
Good/proud: 19
OK/satisfied: 8
More time and it would have been better: 2
Not proud: 3
Hard but fun: 1
Somewhat satisfied: 1
Lazy: 1
Normal: 1
Indifferent: 1

2. Did this project change your attitude of what you are capable of producing? Explain.
No: (already know): 25
Yes: 13

3. Do you think this project impacted how well you learned the content of the Vietnam experience? (Do you think the project affected your performance on the exam?) Explain.
Yes: (learned more than just facts): 29
No: 6
Same as other projects: 3

4. What did you learn about yourself in this process?
    Procrastinator: 11
    If work hard = good job: 9
    (plus a whole variety of random comments)

5. How did the project affect your view on your ability to play the role of an historian?
    Strengthened: 11
    No affect: 10
    Enjoy depth: 3
    Being historian is hard: 2
    It's not so boring: 1
    Everyone can be one: 1
    Like overviews: 1

Appendix 6.3 — Student Focus Group Questions

1. How do you think time should be used in block periods?

2. Do you feel your teachers use it well? Explain.

3. Would you rather:
   Cover more material in less detail?
   Cover fewer topics in more detail?
   Why for which?

4. Do you think this project structure would work with other topics? Explain.

5. Would you rather read, do some worksheets, take test, etc.? Explain.

APPENDIX 6.4 — TEACHER FOCUS GROUP QUESTIONS

Overall Question: How do you strike a balance between depth and coverage in the block period?

1. What do you think is the impact of the block period on depth versus coverage?

2. What is your opinion about the depth versus coverage balance? How do you approach this in your own classes?

3. What are the advantages of depth?

4. What do we give up when we go into depth? Is that acceptable?

5. What kind of balance should we strive for in a U.S. history survey class?

APPENDIX 6.5 — PARENT QUESTIONNAIRE

In the note I sent home at the beginning of our Vietnam project I mentioned this questionnaire. If you could take a few minutes to respond to the following questions, I would appreciate it. Your answers will help me evaluate the effectiveness of the project we have just completed.

1. What is your overall reaction to the project? (positive; negative; explain)
   Good project/positive reaction: 26
   Good to talk about this: 7

2. What seemed to be your student's attitude towards the project? Did this change over time?
   Interested: 18
   Under time crunch (with other work): 3
   Did it because had to: 3
   Interview was interesting: 2
   Curious: 1
   Fine: 1

3. How did this attitude compare to other work (from this class or others)?
   Same: 14
   Better: 8
   A little better: 1

4. Given the fact that such a project takes a significant amount of time, it means that we will cover less material over the year. Based on what you have seen regarding this project, do you believe this is an acceptable trade-off? Please explain.
   Yes: 29
   Maybe: 2

APPENDIX 6.6 — PARENT LETTER

April 10, 1997

Dear Parent/Guardian,

In U.S. history we are undertaking a study of the Vietnam War experience. Your student will be participating in a project that explores this experience in some depth, and will include both an interview, and analyses of primary documents and personal reactions to the war. Your student can show you a copy of the assignment.

I want to look at the impact of such a project on student learning and, to this end, I will be requesting your input regarding your perception of the project's impact on your student. If you could be aware of his or her work on the project, it would be a great help.

When the students have completed the project, I will ask them to have you look at their product and respond to a brief questionnaire. This will take place in the beginning to middle of May. If you have any questions, feel free to call me (204-3280). I appreciate your time and assistance.

Sincerely,

Chris Drape
U.S. History

7

INSTRUCTIONAL STRATEGIES IN THE BLOCK-PERIOD ENGLISH CLASSROOM: THE ROLE OF STUDENT INDEPENDENCE

Pat Hegarty
Shorewood High School

In his ninth grade English class, Pat Hegarty wanted to explore the relative value and effectiveness of three key teaching and learning strategies as perceived both by his students and himself. The strategies were lecture, discussion, and writing workshop.

Hegarty discovered that while each strategy has its value and uses, both he and his students find the writing workshop to be most effective for the kinds of learning and productivity demanded by the assignment of a literary essay based on *Romeo and Juliet*. Hegarty's conclusion is that the power of the writing workshop lies in the "almost complete though organized freedom" it offers to students. He explains, "…at least to some extent, the more independence I allowed, the greater the effectiveness of the strategy, both in the mind of the adolescent and in the view of the instructor." Hegarty notes, however, that at times his students seek the comfort of their predictable and safe dependence on the teacher.

In his reflection, Pat Hegarty also reminds us of the significant challenge the block period presents even to veteran teachers who wish to use it to good advantage. "I see the possibilities presented by the block period," he explains, "but I am still focusing on my old strategies. Time to move on."

RESEARCH SETTING

Shorewood High School is in the Shoreline School District, a mostly suburban community directly north of Seattle. Shorewood is a comprehensive high school composed of grades 9–12, with an enrollment of about 1,700 students. Approximately 90% of Shorewood students go on to further schooling, with 46% enrolling in four-year colleges and universities. Shorewood has changed to a block-period schedule, and for the past 3 years we have had an ABC schedule: 4 days of three 105-minute periods ("A" days and "B" days) and 1 day of 50+-minute periods ("C" days).

ARTICULATING THE RESEARCH QUESTION

This research grew out of my participation in a previous action-research project based on our block-period teaching/learning schedule at Shorewood (see Marshak, D. *Action Research on Block Scheduling,* Larchmont, NY: Eye on Education, 1997). This first project, which we conducted throughout the 1995–96 school year, focused on gaining an understanding of how teaching strategies have changed for us as a result of teaching in 100-minute periods. At the same time, it also examined what these changes might tell us about teachers' values regarding what leads to learning.

A number of issues arose from that research that begged for further study, the most important of which for me was the seeming disparity between what our teachers said they value about teaching in block periods and what our students described as occurring within the classroom. The teachers we interviewed asserted that "...class discussion, library time, group work, independent work, student presentations, use of technology, and simulations are all strategies that appear to work better in the 100-minute period than in the other." Yet when we asked students for their perceptions about how teachers pattern their teaching strategies in block periods at Shorewood, they ranked lecture as the dominant form of instruction, a strategy classified as one of the least effective in the block period. We concluded in our earlier research:

> It is obvious that our sense of what happens in the block-period classroom is sometimes quite different from that of our students, and this knowledge must serve as a vehicle to have us reconsider how we are delivering education, as well as how we are being perceived by those who sit in our classrooms.

Given this conclusion, I determined that it was time to look at my own classroom practices in block periods, from the perspective of my 14 years experience in the classroom. On reflection, I found that there were many good teaching strategies that I employ, but I wanted to clarify what strategy had what effects. What do I do in the classroom that maximizes learning for students? What do I do to reach the most students in a meaningful way?

Another concern I had as I worked through articulating the question was the issue of passion for the subject matter being taught. As teachers we know that our intensity of feeling for a subject impacts how we approach the task of teaching something. So in planning for this study, I was conscious of making sure that I could resonate with passion for the subject matter. For example, when I first began to consider this study we were reading *The Hobbit* in the ninth grade class that I would use as the research setting, and for that book I have enormous passion. I think my students' scores on tests reflected that passion, as did their discussions in class and their work on simple essays. For the actual study I was concerned that a lack of passion for the subject matter might bias the results, so my choice of curriculum subject matter had to be one where I would feel excitement about the content involved.

THE RESEARCH QUESTION

Given three instructional strategies that I use frequently —lecture, discussion, and writing workshop—what is the relative effectiveness of these strategies in promoting learning for my students in the 100-minute period, as perceived by me and by my students?

THE RESEARCH SETTING: ENGLISH 9, PERIOD 2

There are a number of high school teachers who will do whatever it takes not to have to teach freshmen. I am not one of them. I relish the challenges that freshmen present, thrill in their energy, and enjoy enormously the remarkable growth that occurs for so many of them over the course of the year. Some teachers also balk at the lack of intellectual vigor the ninth grade curriculum presents; and it is true that we often spend a good portion of our time working on fundamental skills, especially in writing. This is a challenge I find exciting to tackle and, in my experience, once we get some of these issues fairly well dealt with, there is a lot that we can do together that is intellectually satisfying.

The curriculum in the ninth grade English classroom at Shorewood is quite traditional. In writing instruction, this often means helping students achieve a unity and focus to their writing, while also emphasizing trying a wide variety of written forms. It means paying attention to writing conventions. It means increasing fluency through journal writing and emphasizing the writing process. In my classes, it also means using the computer as an aid throughout the writing process, especially in revising, editing, and publishing.

In addition to working on writing, much of the English 9 curriculum is devoted to literary studies. Public speaking and presentation make up a smaller part of the content. In literary studies, we read a variety of forms, with special attention to learning the vocabulary of literature. Throughout the curriculum there is the continual overlapping of skills between writing and literary studies (Appendix 7.1, p. 176).

In my classes I pay particular attention to this overlapping of writing and literature. While I started my teaching life as a literature lover, I have become more of a composition/ writing instructor as the years have progressed, because I see that this is what young people need most: the ability to articulate their ideas in clear and meaningful ways. My students know that I laughingly, yet consistently, promote my three biases about writing: their writing should be focused and organized, should be mechanically brilliant, and should sound like them (an emphasis on developing the individual voice). My students spend a great deal of time working through a thorough writing process, because my assignments model developing a piece of writing from prewriting through publishing. My students also use computers extensively.

The unit that I chose as the focus for this study featured composition and literary studies and is the final coming together of those elements for the year. The project, a basic literary analysis essay based on Shakespeare's *Romeo and Juliet*, emphasized the simplest use of literary terms and devices, while also pushing the students into the realm of wrestling with the ideas in the play and their meaning beyond the page and beyond the Bard's time. In addition, the project cemented the ideas about writing we had been working on from September: focusing and organizing ideas, developing the individual voice, practicing writing conventions, employing the writing process, and using the computer as an aid (Appendix 7.2, p. 180).

This particular class featured a range of abilities and interests. Of the 33 students in the class, 6 failed; 16 earned scores of A and A–. If anything, this was an unusually strong group, and we enjoyed a healthy rapport, though it took the whole year for this to gel.

Over the course of the school year the students became quite practiced at writing focused pieces in the expository mode. As a result, the students were pretty well schooled in the type of endeavor we were undertaking in this assignment, though in this piece we were taking writing and thinking to yet another level in terms of how the students were asked to articulate ideas.

THE RESEARCH PROCESS

After reflecting on the unit on *Romeo and Juliet* and considering the project which students would complete, I selected three teaching strategies that would serve as the foundation for my research. These three—lecture/direct instruction, writing workshop, and class discussion—were the primary vehicles for generating the essay, and they were also the three most frequently used strategies in my repertoire. For each teaching strategy, I concerned myself with two indicators of effectiveness in promoting learning for my students in the 100-minute block period: the degree to which the students were engaged and on task as a result of the activity, and the attitudes students held regarding the effectiveness of each of the teaching strategies.

LECTURE

The lecture on which I focused was the introductory lecture for the paper that students were going to write. It served three purposes. I wanted to revisit our many discussions on developing individual theme statements about a work of art, while at the same time demonstrating how this statement might be used as the controlling thesis for an essay. The lecture also explained how a formal literary analysis essay should be constructed and introduced the assignment in its formal iteration on paper. The lecture covered both old material and new information.

I asked our audiovisual technician to videotape the lecture, advising him to focus on the students rather than on me. My hope was to see the degree to which they were engaged and on task as I conducted my lecture, and also to gain a sense of how well they enjoyed the experience. In addition, students completed a feedback form about the lecture at the end of the period, the Essay Lecture Evaluation Form (Appendix 7.3, p. 181). On the form students were asked to rate the lecture on a scale and to add comments as explanation.

Finally, as with the other two teaching strategies under investigation, at the end of the unit students filled out another feedback sheet comparing the three different teaching strategies (Appendix 7.4, p. 181). The students rank-ordered the three teaching strategies. Then they indicated the percentage of time that they believed each teaching strategy should be used within the context of this type of learning activity.

WRITING WORKSHOP

The writing workshop's purpose was to allow students time to work on their writing in an atmosphere that encouraged independence and collaboration. While relatively freewheeling, it was still a controlled environment, with the teacher supporting students in working through the writing process, but also demanding focus and productivity from them. In my classes, the writing workshop typically took place in a computer writing lab. All final written work must be typed, and because of the types of peer commenting processes I required from students, it was expected that the work be completed during the writing workshop (Appendix 7.5, p. 182).

In this case, the writing workshop day came several days after the lecture, and the students were asked to come to class with a two-page handwritten draft already completed. (A computer-crafted piece was also acceptable.) Throughout the 100-minute period, I conducted a detailed scan of the room every 15 minutes, noting the number of students actively engaged in either their own text or that of a peer. As with the lecture, at the end of the period students completed an evaluation form about this activity. At the end of the unit, students ranked the effectiveness of the writing workshop in relation to the other two forms of instruction (Appendix 7.6, p. 183).

DISCUSSION

With the help of a colleague I focused on two different class discussions about the play *Romeo and Juliet*. Both discussions preceded the introduction of the paper assignment, though they served as touch points later on as students developed ideas and supporting data for their essays. The first discussion lasted about 30 minutes and focused on identifying the attributes of the various characters: who was appealing, who was not. The second discussion, which lasted approximately 40 minutes, focused on the choices the people in the play made and, by extension, on the choices we make in our lives.

My colleague, a veteran English teacher, sat in on both class discussions and took notes on what she saw in terms of student engagement and attention to task as well as of student affect. Later, we compared notes. Finally, at the end of the unit, the students completed the Ranking Teaching Strategies worksheet (Appendix 7.4, p. 181).

FINDINGS AND ANALYSIS

LECTURE

The standard rap against the lecture is that it is often much too long. Unless the subject matter is of the utmost importance to the student and/or the lecturer is a master of his or her content to the extent that the lecturer is a master salesman of the content, the lecture is a hard sell. Choosing to lecture a class of 14- and 15-year-olds on the structure of a literary essay for 70 minutes might be seen as setting oneself up for failure. At the very least, it was a challenge. In this case it was not a failure, but the students' primary response was predictable: "too long."

As I thought about it after the fact, I agreed. We covered a lot of ground in the 70 minutes, and although students were active in taking notes, responding to questions, and processing ideas together, it was a stretch for them to remain that focused for such a long period of time. However, when I reviewed the tape I was truly amazed at the degree to which they did stay actively engaged. Where I had expected my students to drift and had thought they had, the tape showed them hanging in and hanging on (kicking and screaming, in some cases, and prodded into attention by the teacher in others, but still with it nonetheless). Where I had expected to see students dancing in the aisles when my back was turned, instead I saw them checking each other's notes for accuracy. True, they were not exactly riveted by the content, but they remained engaged.

In the students' feedback forms, lecture lost, coming in at number three. In this ranking of teaching strategies, 70% of the group suggested that I should not allot lecture any more than 30 minutes of class time at one sitting. And yet, having aired this, their responses on the lecture evaluation recognized that this form of instruction is a necessary evil. When asked if they found this lecture engaging, 60% ranked it a 3 or higher on a 5-point scale. When asked if this form of instruction shared the information in an understandable way, a whopping 95% gave the lecture a score of 3 or higher. Finally, when asked if the lecture gave clear directions for moving forward and a clear understanding of how the essay fit into the general context of writing experiences for the class, 90% of the students again responded with a score of 3 or higher.

This mixed-bag of data was surprising, and to some extent, uplifting. I already knew that I am a strong lecturer. However, I was not prepared for how well students seemed to respond to the lecture, both on the tape and in their responses on feedback forms. Both methods of feedback showed that many students had discovered two very important ideas: lectures really should not last 70 minutes, and that when done well, lectures can provide a sound basis for clarifying and directing work that is later done independently. On the other hand, the danger is that lectures will be less effective in meeting student needs when the relevance and importance of the content is not clear and explicit, and when the timing of lecture tends to go on beyond a reasonable limit.

WRITING WORKSHOP

The writing workshop took place a couple of days after the initial lecture. On that date 28 students were in attendance, and every 15 minutes over the course of the period I noted the number of students engaged in the types of activities dictated by the writing workshop. Students were considered on task if they were actively working on their own writing or that of a peer. The scanning involved a periodic glance, followed by a note. While I had paced around the room during the lecture, essentially managing the class by walking around, in the case of the writing workshop I offered little at all in terms of behavioral intervention, acting only to answer questions regarding the writing of the essays.

Over the course of the period, the students in my class showed a very high degree of engagement in the task. At the first check all of the students were actively focused on their work. Subsequent checks showed 3, 4, 4, and 6 students off-task, respectively, while at the final check, 10 minutes before the end of the period, all students were engaged.

On the feedback forms students gave very high marks to the writing workshop activity. Eighty-six percent of the group stated, to a score of 4 or 5, that this activity encouraged engagement in their work. Similarly, 81% agreed, to the score of 4 or 5, that the activity met their needs in terms of what they needed to do to complete the assignment. Thus, on the surface, students appeared to know, understand, and appreciate the value of processing their written work through this type of workshop.

However, the feedback forms also revealed a tremor of dissatisfaction. While students clearly stayed engaged, the feedback forms suggested that two aspects of this activity could be improved. Fully a third of the class gave the item that questioned whether or not the activity provided a direction for moving to the next step a score of 3—not stellar! Similarly, on the item that asked whether or not the workshop format gives meaningful feedback on this type of writing, a third of the group gave the activity a score of 3. Worse though, 18% gave the activity a score of 1 or 2!

These two problems aside, students did rank the writing workshop as the most effective of the three activities under discussion. Two-thirds of the group suggested that this format is best when 30 to 60 minutes are allotted to the activity, while 20% suggested 50 minutes. Twenty-five percent of the students wanted no more than 20 minutes of writing workshop.

This is a strategy that I have practiced and thought I had perfected over the years, but the student feedback offers a new view of the workshop. Clearly students enjoy the independence and focus of the activity; they like the chance to work by themselves, or with a peer, in a purposeful way that gets the work done. On the other hand, the modest scores that the students gave to the questions regarding the activity providing direction and meaningful feedback give me reason to fine-tune the activity.

Part of the problem lies in the tension that we all feel between dependence and independence. Students enjoy the independence of freely pursuing the completion of the task, but they chafe at the reality that the teacher is somewhat out of the picture in this process. It is not always ideal to have the teacher so thoroughly disengaged. For my part, I want them to learn to make choices independent of me and to encourage them to look to each other for answers. Many adolescents don't always want this degree of independence. In short, my freshmen students want the independence and autonomy to create, but they also want my authority around to help with the final production.

DISCUSSION

This tension between dependence and independence has always been a concern for me when I consider class discussion as a teaching strategy. Discussion is the strategy I used most as a beginning teacher, or wanted to use the most, but it has become less of a force in my teaching in recent years. Thus, it was interesting for me to discover in our first study on the 100-minute period, that Shorewood teachers noted the particular effectiveness of class discussions as a teaching strategy in block periods.

When I led the two discussions for this study, I had a colleague, another veteran English teacher, sit in and take notes about what she saw in terms of student engagement, affect, and attention to task. The first discussion lasted about 30 minutes and focused on identifying and exploring the attributes of the various characters in the play: who was appealing, who was not. The second discussion, which lasted approximately 40 minutes, focused on the choices the people in the play made, and, by extension, on the choices we make in life in general.

In a later comparison of notes, I found I was much harsher in my criticism of the teaching/learning than was my colleague. My own notes were riddled with my concerns about how one goes about constructing a discussion. How much do you control? How much independence do you allow? I felt that both class discussions tended to get out of hand easily and then dwindle quickly once things got interesting. In my recollection, I didn't see the work as all that engaging over a significant period of time, and I noted that the nature of the class discussion can allow nontalkers to zone-out easily. Though great ideas were shared in both sessions and students obviously gained something from the discussions, I wrote them off as having severely limited usefulness as an instructional tool.

On the other hand, my colleague found them well planned! From her vantage point at the rear of the classroom she noted that a lot of students were engaged significantly in the dialogue, though they were not actively contributing. She advised me that I should not take too lightly the attention of those who choose not to speak; quiet, she asserted, is not necessarily indicative of a lack of attention, engagement, or interest. She noted my "masterful flexibility": being able to take an idea that a student raises unexpectedly, honor it, make sense of it, and then bring it back to the larger theme under discussion. My colleague said I had an "honest rapport" with my students, enabling me to draw them into the discussion even though they might seem somewhat unwilling. At the same time, she did suggest that I try to stick to a firmer time limit when engaging a group in a discussion.

When ranking the various teaching strategies, my students placed class discussion second to the writing workshop. Two-thirds of the class suggested that the ideal time frame for a discussion is between 30 and 50 minutes, a range that I now find myself reasonably comfortable with, although I think I tend more toward the half hour as the ideal length.

My students' interest in class discussions surprised me. It has always seemed such a chore to get the conversation going, and so I was heartened and surprised to gain such a positive response from my colleague, and such a high rating from my students. Clearly, brevity and focus are key concerns, as in the case of the lecture, and, similarly, the need for establishing a relationship with students that allows for discussion is also a critical attribute. It seems clearer to me now that for this form of teaching strategy to be most effective, it must be clearly and explicitly tied to the larger context of the learning. Often class discussions, at least for me, tend to wander off into the interesting territory of an unusual idea and do not necessarily remain germane to the essential learnings we are exploring. In light of this awareness, one improvement I can make is to make a conscious effort to build specific reflection time into each class discussion, a time in which we can explore in a focused way how the content of our discussion ties into the themes we are studying.

CONCLUSIONS

Through this study I discovered our perceptions of the relative value of these three teaching strategies, at least in terms of this particular assignment. We ranked the three strategies, and the ranking makes sense when we consider all the data together. In the context of our essay on *Romeo and Juliet*, the writing workshop is the best strategy for encouraging the completion of students' work. The students ranked it as the most effective, and true to their preference, they mostly stayed on task and engaged throughout the activity. Class discussion they ranked second, which surprised me, and lecture they placed third, even though they were able to point out its value and uses. But I am left wondering what ideas and insights lurk beneath the immediate findings.

One key theme embedded in all of this is independence. It should come as no surprise that the adolescent is keenly aware of the degree to which she or he controls her or his life, and the degree to which teachers sometimes play the role of learned jailer. In many respects, the problem with lecture is that the student has no control but must sit and passively note the ideas being shared by the teacher. In contrast, the writing workshop allows almost complete, although organized, freedom, including the freedom to do nothing. Somewhere between these two extremes we find the class discussion, which is a more controlled type of freewheeling celebration of ideas, though the teacher is again more in control than the students. In my study, it seems that, at least to some extent, the more independence I allowed, the greater the effectiveness of the strategy, both in the mind of the adolescent and in the view of the instructor.

Having noted this finding, there remains the important reality that the classroom is a community, thus making interdependence, interactivity, collegiality, and collaboration important and necessary ideals. My colleague noted the importance of the relationship that I enjoyed with my students; our easy rapport, to her thinking, allowed a good conversation to take place. On viewing the videotape of the lecture, I have to admit a certain surprised smugness about the same; I was amazed at how long students stayed hooked in, and how this seemed to be more a function of our relationship and less of the fascinating content I was sharing. At the same time, even though the writing workshop was ranked as the most effective strategy, and certainly was the activity in which students stayed most on task, the concerns the students raised about the workshop focused on wanting to have more interaction with and thus dependence on the teacher within this context.

My primary conclusion is hardly revolutionary or new. The direction I need to go as a teacher is to encourage my students' growth toward independence. These young people want to grow up and move beyond needing my lectures, my discussion, my feedback. At the same time, though, the teacher must be careful not to toss the adolescent out with the bath water. I must recognize that although students chafe and bristle at my intervention, they both need it and want it, more as guidance, however, and less as direct, authoritative instruction.

This sounds like simple common sense, and to some extent it is. However, what is challenging to me is that I now realize that I have only a limited number of favored instructional strategies that foster this type of growth. It is not a coincidence that I chose the strategies I did, because they are true to who I am as a teacher; this is how I teach. The realization for me that reverberates from the study is that my repertoire is not great enough, and that to meet the concerns expressed by my students, I must work to expand my cache of teaching strategies.

Do I really use group-work effectively? What of demonstrations and simulations? What about the use of multimedia technologies in presentations, both my own and those of my students? In our first analysis of the work we do in the 100-minute block period, we spoke of all of these as being desired, preferred, and possible now that we have the requisite time. Yet I find myself doing exactly what our earlier research project said we did so well. I see the possibilities presented by the block period, but I am still focusing on my old strategies. Time to move on.

IDEAS FOR NEXT STEPS

In his study, Pat Hegarty looked at both his students' and his own perceptions about the efficacy of three teaching and learning methods in block periods: lecture, class discussion, and writing workshop. His findings suggest several improvements that he could institute in his classroom.

- Be sure to focus a lecture clearly and hold it to 30 minutes at most.

- In writing workshops, provide clear directions to students about the various next steps in the process of completing the assignment at hand. Such directions may need to be provided more than once or in a way that students can access at their discretion; for example, a flow chart on the wall or board.

- Also in writing workshops, provide opportunities for students to receive more immediate feedback about their writing from the teacher. The teacher need not be "somewhat out of the picture" in the writing workshop but can act the role of a resource who does not initiate but is available to respond to students' requests for assistance and a critical reading of their writing. In this manner, the teacher can still promote students' independence while engaged in providing more direct instruction on request. As Hegarty explains, "My freshmen students want the independence and autonomy to create, but they also want my authority around to help with the final production." The teacher's role is to provide for both of these functions in a creative and flexible balance.

- Hegarty might want to experiment with Socratic seminars as a way to encourage student independence and initiative within the context of a whole-class discussion in which the teacher plays an important role. The Socratic seminar form would likely allow him to mediate between his students' desire for independence and for the teacher's authority in a flexible and constructive manner.

APPENDIX 7.1 — ENGLISH 9, SHOREWOOD HIGH SCHOOL: COURSE DESCRIPTION AND EXPECTATIONS

Course Description

The course covers a full year during which the student earns a total of one credit, and satisfies the graduation requirement in English for literature and writing. It is designed to reinforce and to improve language arts skills: writing, speaking, and reading literature.

The writing portion emphasizes writing well-organized compositions using appropriate sentence patterns and well-chosen words. The literature study emphasizes reading in all the essential literary genres—fiction, poetry, drama, and nonfiction. The speech portion is a survey of skills necessary for interpersonal communication, focusing especially on participating in discussions and other speech activities.

Course Objectives

Literature—To develop skills in analyzing setting, characterization, plot development, point of view, theme, tone, atmosphere, irony, foreshadowing, and style. Students will learn to understand literary criticism and write literary papers. They will also learn to recognize how literature reflects historical and cultural influences.

Writing—To write effectively through developing the following concepts: understanding that writing is a process, formulating a controlling thesis, organizing ideas logically and effectively, using convincing supporting evidence and appropriate conclusions, using library research skills, conforming to the basic rules of writing, and using the MLA style of documentation. Students will also work on developing vocabulary.

Speech—To improve interpersonal relations both as a sender and as a receiver. To recognize the importance of adapting the delivery, content, and style of the message to the specific audience.

Washington State Essential Academic Learning Requirements Assessed

The following state Essential Learnings will be emphasized most frequently in this course.

Read with Comprehension—The student understands and uses different skills and strategies to read; the student understands the meaning of what is read; the student reads different materials for a variety of purposes.

Write With Skill—The student writes clearly and effectively; the student writes in a variety of forms for different audiences and purposes; the student understands and uses the steps of the writing process; the student analyzes and evaluates the effectiveness of written work.

Communicate Effectively and Responsibly—The student uses listening and observation skills to gain understanding; the student communicates ideas clearly and effectively; the student uses communication strategies and skills to work effectively with others; the student analyzes and evaluates the effectiveness of communication.

Course Requirements

Reading

Class Reading: As a whole the class will be assigned readings of various lengths, from all literary genres. Students will be expected to complete all reading from the text and supplementary materials as designated. We will be using *Elements of Literature* as our primary text, along with a variety of supplementary texts.

Individual, Out of Class Reading: In addition to class reading, students will be expected to read one or more major works, each semester, outside of class time.

Writing

Major Papers/Projects: In addition to tests and quizzes, we will also undertake a number of projects dealing with broad thematic concepts. All written and project work is expected to meet high standards in the traditional essay format. Our emphasis will be on developing clearly organized, articulate pieces that acknowledge the individual voice, while also meeting rigorous standards.

Journal and Writing Folder: Both a journal and a student writing folder will be maintained, and because you will be writing extensively in our Mac lab, you should also include a Macintosh disk in your class notebook.

Speech

Class Discussions: Every day you will be expected to participate fully in our discussions of the texts we are reading and writing. Participation is essential!

Class Presentations: you will be asked again and again to share your knowledge and expertise with your peers, whether as an expert on a given author or time period, or as a participant in a group project.

Multimedia Presentations: You will find that in this class we will be extending and expanding our traditional definitions of the basic skills noted above as we look to multimedia technologies as ways of expressing ideas.

Grade 9 Minimum product requirements

Literary works:
- Two major works read each semester.
- One or more major works may be required in addition to the class-assigned texts.
- One Shakespearean play, *Romeo and Juliet*, read during the year.

Writing:
- Two expository papers written each semester.
- Writing focuses on preparing students to meet the Essential Learnings.

Oral Communication:
- One stand-up oral presentation prepared and delivered each semester.

Grading Procedures

All assignments are given points with varying total amounts. All work is due on the assigned date. Turning work in on times is essential, as no late work will be accepted. Students will excused absences must complete work immediately upon their return, though some work (group activities, discussion-based assignments) cannot be made up.

The percentage scale for grading all work will be as follows:

A = 100–93%	B- = 82–80%	D+ = 69–67%
A = 92–90%	C+ = 79–77%	D = 66–60%
B+ = 89–87%	C = 76–73%	
B = 86–83%	C- = 72–70%	

Attendance, tardy, discipline policies

With so much time devoted to class participation and in-class composition, punctuality, good attendance, and self discipline are vital to successfully complete this course. This class will follow the district and building attendance policies and guidelines. Tardiness will be recorded and unless excused will prevent the student from completing work missed. Absences will be recorded and will be counted as excused or unexcused according to the building policy.

Additional guidelines for success

See additional teacher handouts for more information.

APPENDIX 7.2 — *ROMEO AND JULIET* THEME PAPER

This assignment emphasizes your making choices about what you'd like to focus on as a culminating writing activity based on your reading of Shakespeare's <u>Romeo and Juliet</u>. I have very specific ideas about what I'd like you to produce.

The goal is for each person to produce a multiple paragraph piece of writing. I'm concerned with the idea of writing a piece that develops your sense of a big idea, or a theme, in the play. In a way, I want you to rant and rave about the play, using **theme** as the vehicle.

In writing this piece I'm interested in seeing how you - YES, YOU! - respond to the play, and as a result, I'm looking for a piece of writing that sounds like you.

Theme
1. Choose a theme that shows up a number of times in the reading of Romeo and Juliet. (Because it is a recurring idea, it is safe to assume that it is and important one!)
2. Develop a theme statement/thesis using the process discussed and practiced in class.
3. Write a literary analysis essay around your theme statement. Write four paragraphs:

- One that explains what you think the author would like us to think about the idea. (Introduction)
- Two paragraphs, each devoted to displaying where this idea plays an important role within the play. (Developmental)
- A paragraph devoted to discussing how/where the big idea works in your life. (Conclusion)

4. Follow the checklist below as our process.

_____	Prewriting - theme development sheet
_____	Two page handwritten draft
_____	Typed draft
_____	Draft read aloud by peer to writer
_____	Final Draft - Highlight one example of each comma rule, and one of each semi-colon rule.

Remember that the two middle paragraphs should be supported with references to the bok. This assignment should be typed, is due at the beginning of the period Tuesday, 6/3/97, and is worth 150 points.

APPENDIX 7.3 — *ROMEO AND JULIET* ESSAY LECTURE EVALUATION

On a scale of 1 - 5, how would you rate today's lecture by your teacher? (One is a very low, score, while 5 is an outstanding score.) Please give a reason in support of your answer.

. . . . in terms of being engaging?

. . . . in terms of sharing information in an understandable way?

. . . . in terms of providing a direction for moving to the next step?

. . . . in terms giving you meaningful information on how this type of writing fits into general writing goals for this class?

APPENDIX 7.4 — RANKING TEACHING STRATEGIES STUDENT RATING RESULTS

Direct Instruction/Lecture

       Rank

Discussion

       Rank

Writing Workshop

       Rank

Appendix 7.5 — Peer Commenting Directions

When you have finished writing, make sure you have saved.

Then, choose anyone from the class and have them sit down at your computer to read and respond to your work. The goal is to have that person offer constructive ideas to help you improve the piece. If something is spelled incorrectly, let them know. If something sounds weird, tell the writer. If you really like something, celebrate it. Make sure your comments are written within parentheses, are bold, and that you have included your initials.

When your partner has finished commenting, make sure s/he has saved the piece.

Then have a second person go through the process.

When the second person has finished, make sure that the piece is saved using the SAVE command. Then, save it again, this time using SAVE AS. This will allow you to save the piece using a separate title. Type in the new title in the window. It should read Lastname RJ Essay Final.

When you click on save you will notice that your document looks the same as it did, but has a new name. Now it is time to clean up.

Get rid of all the comments, taking time to incorporate into your piece the ideas and suggestions you think are most valid. Be sure to follow the titling and font guides we have articulated.

When this is all done save it using the SAVE command, and print out both versions for me - the original , with all the comments within the body of the writing, plus the final, all revised and edited.

APPENDIX 7.6 — *ROMEO AND JULIET* WRITING WORKSHOP EVALUATION

On a scale of 1 - 5, how would you rate today's class? (One is a very low, score, while 5 is an outstanding score.) Please give a reason in support of your answer.

How would you rate today's class?

. . . . in terms of your being engaged in your work?

. . . . in terms of meeting what you needed to do in order to complete your assignment?

. . . . in terms of providing a direction for moving to the next step?

. . . . in terms giving you meaningful feedback on this type of writing?

Did you come to class with your homework prepared?

APPENDIX 7.7 — *ROMEO AND JULIET*
THEMATIC ESSAY EVALUATION

Please attach the final to all original drafts and prewriting pieces of your paper. Then hand all in, and your work will be scored based on the categories and weights below.

Writer   _____

Score   _____

___1___2___3___4___5
Structure (x6)
Does the piece have a sense of wholeness? Does it appear to progress logically, with a clear beginning, a middle, and an end? Or, does it seem to meander awkwardly, without focusing on an idea, or a series of related ideas? Have you worked to use the attention getter, the transition, and the thesis in both the introduction and the conclusion?

___1___2___3___4___5
The assignment, the voice (x4)
Have you covered the basics of the assignment? Have you produced a multiple paragraph piece of writing that develops a sense of a theme? Have you focused on responding to the book? Are the developmental paragraphs supported using references to the play? Do you work to present an authentic voice? Have you studiously avoided the use of first person pronouns?

___1___2___3___4___5
Conventions (x6)
Does this piece conform to standard written English? Has the writer worked to craft a paper that has few mechanical errors? Are the pieces written in complete sentences? Do you use all of our new comma and semi-colon rules?

___1___2___3___4___5
Process (x4)
Are all originals included here?
_____   Prewriting - theme development sheet
_____   Two page handwritten draft
_____   Typed draft
_____   Draft read aloud by peer to writer
_____   Final Draft - Highlight one example of each comma rule, and one of each semi-colon rule.

8

PROMOTING STUDENT ENGAGEMENT: LESSONS FROM THE STUDIES

What are the lessons that teachers can draw from these studies about the opportunities provided by block periods in American high schools?

The central complaint of teachers in high schools is that students don't care enough about school. "Good students" are dutiful, they do their work, and go through the motions of compliance. "Mediocre students" do less. "Bad students" do little or nothing and act out. Many teachers complain that few students are genuinely engaged in the activities conducted in their classrooms, that few students really care about learning. Clichés? Perhaps to some extent, but at the core of these clichés is truth: the conventional high school model does not engage most young people today. Young people's attitudes about school mirror those of their teachers. The most common complaint of high school students is that school is boring and disconnected from the felt experience of their lives.

For both teachers and students the key question is this: Might things be different? Might high school classes more effectively engage young people both in their daily activities and in learning?

STUDENT ENGAGEMENT

The most significant finding of these studies is that many or most high school students can become more deeply engaged in their school work within the context of block-period classes. And these teacher-researchers provide us with examples of how they have promoted increased student engagement in their own classrooms.

Kimberly Allison's study demonstrates that when students work together with a teacher to develop an assessment instrument, many students will be engaged by this activity, because it draws upon and validates their own knowing. It is a meaningful activity, because students see its immediate application. When students develop their own assessment instrument, they are more likely to use the instrument's criteria as they complete the related assignment. And when they use their student-developed assessment tool to assess their own work, they are more likely to care about how good their work is.

Jeannie Wenndorf's study shows that project assessments increase engagement for most students because they integrate four elements: projects are more interesting in and of themselves than tests; projects are group activities and the social element is deeply engaging for most students; projects result in new learning; and projects lead to a greater sense of accomplishment for most students. One insight that encompasses all of these elements is that many students perceive project assessments as fun. Project assessments also result in students devoting more time to their schoolwork than tests do, another measure of increased engagement.

Mark Lovre's study suggests that as students learn to manage in-class project time more effectively, that is, to manage their independence more consciously and productively, they become more successful at completing the work assigned in the course. They become more successful because they become more engaged in class activities, in reading, writing, and talking about the curriculum of this English class. So the increased range of independence provided to students, within a structured framework and with the acquisition of skills for managing that independence, brings the majority of them to an acceptance of greater responsibility, and an increase in their engagement in the class. Lovre's study also underlines the importance of teaching students the skills they need to manage increased independence successfully.

Feather Alexander's study demonstrates how the new responsibility of teaching their peers increases the engagement in class activities of most students. She explains, "Once the students had begun to identify and reflect upon their ability to work together to create and offer a presentation, they began to see their own growth and also found this work to be an enjoyable experience that had merit in terms of their learning."

Alexander further notes that "students said that participation, effort, and involvement by the whole class made learning enjoyable....[T]hey seemed to enjoy the fact that the teaching activities had a positive effect upon overall participation in the classroom." As students took on the challenge of learning how to teach their peers, they constructed a social environment in the class in which they brought positive peer pressure on all students to become more engaged as learners and teachers. "Students felt frustrated and less effective when class participation was not 100%....Most students wanted everyone to succeed, and participation was crucial for understanding, learning, and success."

Kristi Noren's study shows that personalization in the classroom is likely to lead to greater student engagement in classroom activities. In this case, the personalization came through individual goal-setting, fitness-testing data, personalized training programs, and the overall intensification of relationships between students and teacher, all of which became possible within the context of the block period structure. While to some extent Noren likely accomplished her study goals as a result of her small class size, her findings nonetheless argue for teachers to use the block period structure as a vehicle for greater personalization of their teaching, even with larger class sizes.

Chris Drape explains that the project he assigned in his block-period history class "engaged students meaningfully in first-hand historical work. They became the 'doers' instead of the 'receivers.'...The students were engaged enough to work hard and well....I was impressed across the board by the quality and thoughtfulness of their projects. This held for the motivated students who generally do well, as well as for a substantial number of underachievers, who rose to the occasion and met the challenge of this project....There are some subtle, yet important, messages about the importance of giving students more power in their study of history if we seek their meaningful involvement in this enterprise." The block period allowed Drape to provide his students with "more power in their study of history," which led to greater student engagement in their activities as well as higher quality work in Drape's view.

Pat Hegarty's study suggests that structured freedom in the block-period class leads to the greatest amount of student engagement. He notes, "In my study it seems that at least to some extent, the more independence I allowed, the greater the effectiveness of the strategy, both in the mind of the adolescent and in the view of the instructor." And the structure of the block period encouraged him to provide a learning context with increased independence.

STUDENT INITIATIVE

Another finding of these studies is that many high school students can and will take greater initiative in the high school classroom if they are given the proper set of opportunities and incentives.

With project assessments as described by Wenndorf, students needed to take the initiative to conduct and complete their projects. Tests required no such efforts from them.

With the range of independence and the amount of project time provided by Lovre's class system, students needed to take the initiative if they were to be successful within this structure. Lovre's study shows that many students need assistance if they are to be successful in managing the kind of independence he provided for them. They need to develop appropriate skills, and the teacher needs to plan for and lead the students' skill acquisition. Lovre's study also demonstrates that with such skill development, students can both increase their capacity to take initiative and be clearly cognizant of why they are doing this. As one student explained, "This system is great in the way that it forces you to be independent and rely on yourself (much of which is like how next year and college will be like)." Another student noted, "I feel I learn more in most areas of this class because it is up to me to pay attention and it is up to me to ask questions when I don't understand."

With students teaching their peers in Alexander's class, many students understood that all group members had to take some initiative if the group's teaching were to be successful. Once the students began to value their own efforts as teachers, "students started to assume more control of their own learning. They began monitoring each other's behavior in the literature groups, focusing to keep everyone on task. They also began to check and offer revisions on the individual jobs that each group member had done." Students in this class also took initiative in relation to maintaining decorum in the classroom:

> Though disruptions remained a major concern throughout the course, they began to diminish, and the way they were dealt with began to change. ...By the end of the term, students had begun to monitor each other. For example, during the last unit, a student wrote an unsolicited letter to the class expressing her concerns over behavior during the class discussions....The class seemed to consider her request rather than shun it, as they might have done had I simply expressed my own concerns.

Finally, in Noren's study, about half of the students took initiative by increasing their levels of exercise both in class and outside of class.

ASSESSMENT AS LEARNING

A third finding suggested by several of these studies is that many high school students are engaged by an assessment process that goes beyond the boundaries of conventional show-what-you-know testing and becomes another vehicle for learning. Students are even more likely to be engaged when they help to develop the assessment tools themselves.

In Alexander's study, students gave each other feedback about how effectively their teaching efforts had met the criteria for good teaching described in their teaching rubric. Many students attended to this feedback carefully and used it to improve their performance as teachers. The power of this assessment process was enhanced by the fact that the students had created the rubric themselves from their own collective knowledge.

Students developed their own assessment tool in Allison's class as well. They knew more about what was expected of them, because they had helped to develop the assessment. The feedback they received through the student-developed assessment made more sense to them, and they were more interested in learning what it was and how it might be helpful to them. Students were more likely to understand and care about criteria and rules they had helped to create themselves.

In Wenndorf's class, project assessments gave students a richer, more differentiated kind of feedback about their learning than did tests. Students also discovered that the assessment process could generate new learning, not just show what they already knew.

Noren provided students with detailed personalized data about their fitness conditions in terms of body composition (fat percentage), cardiovascular endurance, flexibility, and muscle strength. These data gave students specific targets with which they could measure improvement. While students did not create these assessment tools, they saw the data they received not as some external evaluation of their performance but, rather, as steps in the process of working toward their own goals for increased physical fitness.

One concern often raised in regard to student-developed assessments is the potential limitation in such assessments due to possible student ignorance. Do high school students know enough to establish assessments based on high standards? Another concern lies in the tension between student-developed assessments and district and state curriculum and outcome mandates.

Kimberly Allison provides an answer to such concerns in her discussion of the process she led through which students developed a speech rubric. She engaged the students in developing the elements of the rubric. As she did so, she "was working from a detailed model rubric another teacher had lent me so that I could make sure we covered the essential areas within each component."

Allison modeled a dialogue between her students' knowing and professional standards in her field so that the rubric created embodied elements of both. It was generated primarily from students' knowing, but it included relevant elements that met professional standards. This kind of dialogue could be employed in mediating between any set of external standards in a curricular area and the relevant student-developed criteria.

In summary, the lesson from these studies is that assessment can serve multiple simultaneous functions. Assessment can show learning and generate learning. And it can promote student engagement, particularly when students are involved in developing the tools for assessment. As Allison explains,

> If I create the assessment tool independent of student input, then students are likely to perceive it as lacking connection to their own understanding and/or lacking meaning. If, on the other hand, students help to generate the tool and then use it themselves, they are much more likely to accept and value the criteria and to do what it takes to achieve them. In addition, the connection between the work they do and the grade they receive becomes clear to them, because they have articulated

the expectations themselves, at least to a significant extent.

NEW ROLES, NEW PERCEPTIONS

Finally, two of these studies offer profound lessons for
teachers who seek to engage their high school students more
genuinely and deeply in the activities of their classrooms.
One involves new roles. As Feather Alexander explains,

> ...[A]s time went on and students became more
> successful at teaching each other, I believe that we
> achieved an expansion of our roles that was mark-
> ed by a new balance. Within this balance I gave up
> much or even most of the control of the classroom,
> and my students accepted significantly higher lev-
> els of responsibility for their own learning. Interest-
> ingly, at the same time that I was hesitant to relin-
> quish control of my classroom, my students seemed
> unable to expand their traditional roles within the
> classroom. But by the end of the term, I had let go
> significantly, and they had grown dramatically.

If teachers want students to become more engaged and
demonstrate greater initiative and responsibility, they must
re-vision and re-create their own roles in the classroom in
ways that are coherent with the new roles of more engaged
and empowered learners.

The second lesson has to do with new perceptions: new
perceptions of themselves held by students, and new perceptions of students held by teachers. Chris Drape explains,

> Thirteen (33%) [of the students] said the project
> did affect their views of their own abilities: "I like
> the fact that this showed me that I am able and
> competent to complete a thorough job on a task. It
> may make it easier for similar assignments to
> come." This number is significant if such a change
> has a lasting impact on how these students work in
> the future. For this reason alone, I would argue the
> clear value of this kind of extended project.

Drape's study suggests that by opening up their classroom agendas in block periods in the ways described in Drape's research and the other studies in this volume, teachers can encourage students to act successfully in more empowered and responsible ways. Through their awareness of their success, students can develop enhanced perceptions of their own capabilities. This is not self-esteem separated from experience. Rather, as the student quoted above notes, this is enhanced self-esteem and self-confidence based on the details of accomplishment, on the demonstration of skill and capability and learning and knowledge.

And as students develop the skills and capacities to be "able and competent to complete a thorough job on a task," teachers can gain new perceptions of young people's capacities and learn to expect and nurture even higher levels of competence, engagement, and learning in their students.